Isaac is a gifted eva
wisdom on a subject
souls is evident throu   ....ook that calls everyone
to be born again.

—Dr. Lars Wilhelmsson
Pastor, Author, Part-Time Missionary, and Adjunct
Professor at Alliance Theological Seminary

I have read this book and highly recommend to all the believers in the Lord Jesus Christ to read this book. Be encouraged to buy and teach from this anointed, powerful, and mandated written word.

—Dr. Cedric Richards Sr., Chief Apostle,
Light of the World Deliverance Ministries
International Fellowship

JUST BE BORN AGAIN

THE SUPREME DECLARATION OF THE VISIBLE GOD, JESUS CHRIST

ISAAC KING

CREATION HOUSE

Just Be Born Again by Rev. Isaac William King
Published by Creation House
A Charisma Media Company
600 Rinehart Road
Lake Mary, Florida 32746
www.charismamedia.com

Design Director: Justin Evans
Cover design by Terry Clifton

Visit the author's website: http://www.revisaacwilliamking.com

Library of Congress Cataloging-in-Publication Data: 2014941148
International Standard Book Number: 978-1-62136-768-0
E-book International Standard Book Number:
978-1-62136-769-7

First edition

14 15 16 17 18 — 987654321
Printed in Canada

DEDICATION

To my mother, who labored me in her old age and is living to pray for me until today. Her fervent prayer for me from my birth was and is, "Lord, give my son wisdom like the king Solomon."

Note: I am the only son of her old age after her seven daughters were born. Many saints prayed for my parents to have a son. Everyone believes that I am the answer to their prayers. When my father was a missionary in the northern part of India, my mother worked very hard to take care of my seven sisters. Now she is eighty-nine years old and still praying for me.

As a human being don't try to live like God, the Holy One; but give Him a chance to live in you, so you can be born again to enter into heaven.

CONTENTS

Acknowledgments xi

1 Born Again 1

2 Who Can Save Us from Sin and Hell? 3

3 Jesus Is God 5

4 Law vs. Faith in Christ 17

5 The Love and Grace of God Are Only Found
   in Jesus Christ 18

6 Love vs. Law 20

7 God Is Not Law, but LOVE 24

8 What Is the New Covenant? 27

9 What Is the Work of God That We Must Do? . . 32

10 The Supreme Declaration of the Visible God,
   Jesus Christ 35

11 Why Me? 60

12 Be Sure of Your Salvation 62

13 Evidences of Being Born Again to Enter
   Into Heaven 65

14 Becoming Like Jesus 88

   Notes 95

   Bibliography 97

   About the Author's Ministry 98

   Contact the Author 99

ACKNOWLEDGMENTS

B EFORE I STARTED to write this book, I went to the
Church On The Way in Van Nuys for the first time
for the Annual Conference of the King's University,
where Pastor Robert Morris (Gateway Church) gave the
closing sermon. After the service, an old woman came to
me and told me, "I am a descendant of the Tribe of Ben-
jamin, the Lord told me to tell you. What the Lord gave
you, you know how to do it. He empowered you so you
can finish the job of the Lord. Do it with confidence; the
Lord is with you always." I told her, "Yes, I received it this
year and became the one to do it." The wording was very
personal; only she and I knew what the Lord was talking
about. It is a big story, but the bottom line is to preach
the gospel through the power of the Holy Spirit to win
the lost people. Her prophecy did not only encourage me,
but gave fire in my heart to work hard for the lost souls.
This book will tell some about: "What the Lord gave me,
and I know how to do it, because the Lord recreated me
and empowered me to do it." I believe you will enjoy the
anointing of the Lord when you will read this book to
become the one as He planned for you.

I am happy that the Holy Spirit used me to write
almost half of this book within seven hours on the evening of November 26, 2012. It is my heart's cry to help the
lost souls to be born again through Jesus and His Spirit. I
am grateful to my greatest Teacher, the Holy Spirit, who
has been teaching me since I became born again. He even
wakes me up in the middle of the night to teach me.

I hope and pray that this book will help you to be born

again. I also hope that the Holy Spirit will enable you to serve the lost souls of this world.

I pray that when you are reading this book the Holy Spirit will inspire you to eat and drink from Him where the Living Water will wash all your sins and the Living Spirit will dwell in you to serve the Lord of all lords, the King of all kings.

Just know today, this time is your time of salvation by being born again by the Water and the Spirit. Please be practical to accept the flesh, blood, and soul of Jesus to be truly forgiven from all sins to become holy where you can receive the Spirit of Jesus, the Holy Spirit.

I thank the Lord for the blessings I enjoy to know Him deeply and personally for serving His present kingdom. Lord, You are everything to me. I have drawn deep into Your blood and Spirit to live in You.

I also thank my mentor, Pastor Lars Wilhelmsson; and Stephanie Arena for helping me to edit this book. Thank you for everyone who supported and prayed for me to serve the Lord. I especially thank Dr. Jack Hayford for the impartation of anointing to write for the Lord and His kingdom. I also thank all of my professors who cared so much about me for getting the best from their own life experiences.

With Jesus's love and fellowship through His Spirit, the Holy Spirit,

—REVEREND ISAAC WILLIAM KING

1
BORN AGAIN

BORN AGAIN MEANS saved from sins and judgment, and recreated by the Spirit of God, the Holy Spirit, to live with God forever.

Originally, we can only find the phrase "born again" one time in the whole Bible:

> Jesus answered and said to him, "Most assuredly, I say to you, unless one is born again, he cannot see the kingdom of God."
>
> —JOHN 3:3

Jesus explained in John 3:5 how one can be born again:

> Jesus answered, "Most assuredly, I say to you, unless one is born of water and the Spirit, he cannot enter the kingdom of God."

Peter used the same meaning as Jesus said in John 3:3, 5 that was translated in the New Living Translation:

> All praise to God, the Father of our Lord Jesus Christ. It is by his great mercy that we have been born again, because God raised Jesus Christ from the dead. Now we live with great expectation, and we have a priceless inheritance—an inheritance that is kept in heaven for you, pure and undefiled, beyond the reach of change and decay.
>
> —1 PETER 1:3–4

Actually, "born again" means becoming children of God by receiving new life, the life of the Holy Spirit through Jesus, which we can find in John 1:12–13; 2 Corinthians

5:17; Titus 3:5; 1 Peter 1:3; 1 John 2:29; 3:9; 4:7; 5:1–4, 18. (Please open your own Bible and read each verse.)

The original word for "born again" has another meaning that is "born from above." We will learn both ways to get the truth to be strong in our faith to be born again or born from above/heaven.

Jesus spoke Greek, Aramaic, and Hebrew. He used one of these languages to talk with Nicodemus.

The word *born* is from the Greek word *gennao,* and the Greek word *anothen* was translated as "again" or "from above."

In Aramaic, *metiled* means "born" and the word *toob* means "again." In Aramaic there is another word *d'reesh* that is used instead of *toob,* which means "from above." Both of these words are translated in Greek as *anothen.* The Aramaic word *Metiled d'reesh* has another meaning that is "born as the beginning from above" or "becoming as the beginning once again."

The Hebrew word *yivvaled* means "be born" and the word *milma'əlah* means "from above."

> Therefore, if anyone is in Christ, he is a new creation; old things have passed away; behold, all things have become new.
>
> —2 CORINTHIANS 5:17

Many believers of Christ also experience being born again as new life or everlasting life or eternal life.

Everything we will know from this book is about being born again for our personal experience with God where we can hear His voice to obey Him for living and serving His kingdom. And finally we can live with God in heaven forever.

2
WHO CAN SAVE US FROM SIN AND HELL?

O NLY GOD CAN save us from sin and hell. Only God is worthy of worship, for He alone is holy. The Hebrew prophet Isaiah called Him "The Holy One of Israel, the Messiah, the anointed One of God who would come to redeem His people." In Isaiah we can find twenty-five times "The Holy One of Israel," in Hebrew "K'dosh Yisrael" in different verses. His glorious reign would bring the blessing of salvation to all the earth (Isa. 11:1–16) and light to those who lived in spiritual darkness (Isa. 9:1–2). His name is Immanuel, which means God with us. In 740 BC Isaiah prophesied, "All right then, the Lord himself will give you the sign. Look! The virgin will conceive a child! She will give birth to a son and will call him Immanuel (which means 'God is with us')" (Isa. 7:14).

Jesus is the Holy One of Israel who only was born on earth through a virgin. That is why Matthew 1:21–23 says, "'She [Virgin Mary] will give birth to a son, and you are to give him the name Jesus, because he will save his people from their sins.' All this took place to fulfill what the Lord had said through the prophet: 'The virgin will conceive and give birth to a son, and they will call him Immanuel' (which means 'God with us')" (NIV).

The Old Testament says that God is Spirit, doesn't it? What did the Hebrew prophet Isaiah say?

> For unto us a Child is born, unto us a son is given;
> and the government will be upon His shoulder.

3

> And His name will be called *Wonderful, Counselor, Mighty God, Everlasting Father, Prince of Peace.* Of the increase of His government and peace there will be no end, upon the throne of David and over His kingdom, to order it and establish it with judgment and justice from that time forward, even forever. The zeal of the LORD of hosts will perform this.
>
> —ISAIAH 9:6–7, EMPHASIS ADDED

So, Jesus is *the Wonderful Counselor, the Mighty God, the Everlasting Father, and the Prince of Peace.*

Prophet Isaiah did not only talk about the virgin birth of the Holy One of Israel, but also talked about His sufferings in chapter 53, as a suffering servant who took all our sins in order to save us. Only God who is the Holy One of Israel, the Lord God of Israel, the King of Israel (Ps. 89:18), and the suffering servant of Israel can save us from sin and hell. Jesus is the only person who holds all these titles. He is the Holy One of Israel. So we can only be saved through Jesus; only Jesus can save us from sin and hell. The Hebrew word *Yeshua* (English "Jesus") means the "Savior." Who can neglect this only Savior of the whole mankind?

Summary: Our God is the only One who can save us, and His name is *Jesus*, because Jesus hosted the Father and the Spirit in His human body as the Son of God, and became visible to us as the Living God. (Please read John chapter 1.)

3
JESUS IS GOD

W HERE IN THE Bible did Jesus claim to be God? Yeshua (Jesus) said:

> "I said to you that you shall die in your sins, for unless you shall believe that I AM THE LIVING GOD, you shall die in your sins."
>
> —JOHN 8:24, ABPE

> Yeshua said to him, "I AM THE LIVING GOD, The Way and The Truth and The Life; no man comes my Father but by me alone. If you had known me, you also would have known my Father, and from this hour you do know him and you have seen him." Philippus said to him, "Our Lord, show us The Father, and it is sufficient for us." Yeshua said to him, "All this time I am with you and you have not known me Philip? Whoever has seen me has seen The Father, and how do you say, 'Show us The Father?' Do you not believe that I am in my Father and my Father in me? The words which I am speaking, I am not speaking from myself, but my Father who dwells within me, he does these works. Believe that I am in my Father and my Father in me, otherwise believe because of the works"
>
> —JOHN 14:6–11, ABPE

In John 10:30–33, Jesus said, "The Father and I are one." The Jewish leaders picked up rocks again to stone Him to death. Jesus said to them, "I have shown you many good deeds from the Father. For which one of them are you going to stone me?" The Jewish leaders replied, "We are not going to stone you for a good deed but for blasphemy, because you, a man, are claiming to be God."

When Satan came to test Jesus, he found the original test of God and fled away from Him. Satan said to Jesus:

> "If You are the Son of God, throw Yourself down. For it is written: 'He shall give His angels charge over you,' and, 'In their hands they shall bear you up, lest you dash your foot against a stone.'" Jesus said to him, "It is written again, 'You shall not tempt the LORD your God.'"
>
> —MATTHEW 4:6–7

Finally, Jesus said that He is God, and Satan ran away from Him. Here Jesus proved 100 percent that He is God, and Satan must not come to test Him by seeing His human body.

> And without controversy great is the mystery of godliness:
> *God was manifested in the flesh,*
> Justified in the Spirit,
> Seen by angels,
> Preached among the Gentiles,
> Believed on in the world,
> Received up in glory.
>
> —1 TIMOTHY 3:16, EMPHASIS ADDED

This is Jesus Christ our Lord, God, Savior, and King.

> "Behold, the virgin shall be with child, and bear a Son, and they shall call His name Immanuel," which is translated, "God with us."
>
> —MATTHEW 1:23

HOW DO WE KNOW THAT JESUS IS GOD?

God is the Creator

> In the beginning God created the heavens and the earth.
>
> —GENESIS 1:1

Thus says the LORD, your Redeemer, and He who formed you from the womb: "I am the LORD, who makes all things, who stretches out the heavens all alone, who spreads abroad the earth by Myself."

—ISAIAH 44:24

Jesus is the Creator

All things were made through Him [Jesus], and without Him [Jesus] nothing was made that was made.

—JOHN 1:3

For by Him all things were created that are in heaven and that are on earth, visible and invisible, whether thrones or dominions or principalities or powers. All things were created through Him and for Him.

—COLOSSIANS 1:16

God is "I AM"

And God said to Moses, "I AM WHO I AM." And He said, "Thus you shall say to the children of Israel, 'I AM has sent me to you.'"

—EXODUS 3:14

Jesus is "I AM"

Jesus said to them, "Most assuredly, I say to you, before Abraham was, I AM."

—JOHN 8:58

(See also Mark 6:50, 14:62; Matt. 14:27; John 13:19, 18:5–6, 22:70.)

God never changes

For I am the LORD, I do not change.

—MALACHI 3:6

Jesus never changes

Jesus Christ is the same yesterday, today, and forever.

—HEBREWS 13:8

God is the first and the last

"I, the LORD, am the first; and with the last I am He."

—ISAIAH 41:4

Jesus is the first and the last

[Jesus said] "I am the First and the Last."

—REVELATION 1:17

God has life in Himself

For as the Father has life in Himself.

—JOHN 5:26A

Jesus has life in Himself

So He [Father] has granted the Son [Jesus] to have life in Himself.

—JOHN 5:26B

In Him was life, and the life was the light of men.

—JOHN 1:4

[Jesus said] "I lay down My life that I may take it again. No one takes it from Me, but I lay it down of Myself. I have power to lay it down, and I have power to take it again."

—JOHN 10:17–18

God is one, there is none like Him

Hear, O Israel: The LORD our God, the LORD is one!

—DEUTERONOMY 6:4

Jesus, His Father, and His Spirit are One God; there is none like Jesus

"I [Jesus] and My Father are one."

—JOHN 10:30

"He who has seen Me [Jesus] has seen the Father."

—JOHN 14:9

> For there are three that bear witness in heaven: the Father, the Word, and the Holy Spirit; and these three are one.
>
> —1 JOHN 5:7

God is the Holy One

> And such as have escaped of the house of Jacob, will never again depend on him who defeated them, but will depend on the LORD, the Holy One of Israel, in truth.
>
> —ISAIAH 10:20

> Also with the lute I will praise You—and Your faithfulness, O my God! To You I will sing with the harp, O Holy One of Israel.
>
> —PSALM 71:22

Jesus is the Holy One

> And the angel answered and said to her, "The Holy Spirit will come upon you, and the power of the Highest will overshadow you; therefore, also, that Holy One who is to be born will be called the Son of God.
>
> —LUKE 1:35

> For You will not leave my soul in Hades, nor will You allow Your Holy One [Jesus] to see corruption.
>
> —ACTS 2:27

> The God of Abraham, Isaac, and Jacob, the God of our fathers, glorified His Servant Jesus, whom you delivered up and denied in the presence of Pilate, when he was determined to let Him go. But you denied the Holy One [Jesus] and the Just, and asked for a murderer to be granted to you, and killed the Prince of life, whom God raised from the dead, of which we are witnesses.
>
> —ACTS 3:13–15

> And that He raised Him from the dead, no more to return to corruption, He has spoken thus: "I will give

you the sure mercies of David." Therefore He also
says in another Psalm: "You will not allow Your Holy
One to see corruption."

—Acts 13:34–35

God forgives the sinner's sins and heals

When Jesus saw their faith, He said to the paralytic,
"Son, your sins are forgiven you"…"Who can forgive
sins but God alone?"

—Mark 2:5, 7

[God] Who forgives all your iniquities, who heals all
your diseases.

—Psalm 103:3

Jesus forgives the sinner's sins and heals

When Jesus saw their faith, He said to the paralytic,
"Son, your sins are forgiven…But that you may know
that the Son of Man has power on earth to forgive
sins."

—Mark 2:5, 10

He [Jesus] cast out the spirits with a word, and healed
all who were sick.

—Matthew 8:16

God is the only Savior

I, even I, am the Lord, And besides Me there is no
savior.

—Isaiah 43:11

But showing all good fidelity, that they may adorn the
doctrine of God our Savior in all things.

—Titus 2:10

For to this end we both labor and suffer reproach,
because we trust in the living God, who is the Savior
of all men, especially of those who believe.

—1 Timothy 4:10

And my spirit has rejoiced in God my Savior.

—Luke 1:47

Jesus is the only Savior

And she will bring forth a Son, and you shall call His name JESUS, for He will save His people from their sins.

—MATTHEW 1:21

Nor is there salvation in any other, for there is no other name under heaven given among men by which we must be saved.

—ACTS 4:12

Then the angel said to them, "Do not be afraid, for behold, I bring you good tidings of great joy which will be to all people. For there is born to you this day in the city of David a Savior, who is Christ the Lord."

—LUKE 2:10–11

And we have seen and testify that the Father has sent the Son as Savior of the world.

—1 JOHN 4:14

Simon Peter, a bondservant and apostle of Jesus Christ, to those who have obtained like precious faith with us by the righteousness of our God and Savior Jesus Christ.

—2 PETER 1:1

But grow in the grace and knowledge of our Lord and Savior Jesus Christ. To Him be the glory both now and forever. Amen.

—2 PETER 3:18

"Now we believe, not because of what you said, for we ourselves have heard Him and we know that this is indeed the Christ, the Savior of the world."

—JOHN 4:42

Therefore I endure all things for the sake of the elect, that they also may obtain the salvation which is in Christ Jesus with eternal glory.

—2 TIMOTHY 2:10

And having been perfected, He [Jesus] became the
author of eternal salvation to all who obey Him.

—Hebrews 5:9

Grace, mercy, and peace from God the Father and the
Lord Jesus Christ our Savior.

—Titus 1:4

Only God is worshipped

For it is written, "You shall worship the Lord your
God, and Him only you shall serve."

—Matthew 4:10

Jesus is worshipped

While He [Jesus] spoke these things to them, behold,
a ruler came and worshiped Him [Jesus], saying, "My
daughter has just died, but come and lay Your hand
on her and she will live."

—Matthew 9:18

But when He again brings the firstborn [Jesus] into
the world, He says: "Let all the angels of God worship
Him [Jesus]."

—Hebrews 1:6

And Thomas answered and said [worshipped] to Him
[Jesus], "My Lord and my God!"

—John 20:28

The human body of Jesus was not only conceived by His
(the Father's) Holy Spirit, but was a visible shell/temple
that actually housed the Father. God was in Christ, "rec-
onciling the world to Himself" (2 Cor. 5:19). Jesus was the
fullness of God to live with us bodily as "Immanuel." His
name is Immanuel (Matt. 1:23). Jesus is the only visible
true and living God for the whole universe.

Jesus is the Son of God too, because God the Father
called Jesus His Son (Matt. 3:17), because the angel
Gabriel declared Jesus the Son of God (Luke 1:35).

> And suddenly a voice came from heaven, saying, "This is My beloved Son, in whom I am well pleased."
>
> —MATTHEW 3:17

> And the angel answered and said to her, "The Holy Spirit will come upon you, and the power of the Highest will overshadow you; therefore, also, that Holy One who is to be born will be called the Son of God."
>
> —LUKE 1:35

If Jesus is God and hosted His Father in Him as well as the Holy Spirit, then why did He say that His Father is greater than Him?

It is only possible in the Trinity. One member can be subordinate to the other two members for a short period of time for a greater purpose that does not change the substance of God from any of the three members of the Godhead.

> The function of one member of the Trinity may for a time be subordinate to one or both of the other members, but that does not mean he is in any way inferior in essence. Each of the three persons of the Trinity as had, for a period of time, a particular function unique himself. This is to be understood as a temporary role for the purpose of accomplishing a given end, not a change in status or essence.[1]

When Jesus said His Father is greater than Him (John 14:28, Mark 10:18, and other places) it ultimately glorified the Godhead. The Son also did not become less than the Father through incarnation, but He subordinated Himself to accomplish His mission according to the Father's will. In addition, Jesus subordinated Himself not to tell us the specific date and time of the future events like the second coming and the final judgment for good purposes.

In the case of "unpardonable sin" the Holy Spirit is greater than the Father and the Son.

> So I tell you, every sin and blasphemy can be forgiven—except blasphemy against the Holy Spirit, which will never be forgiven. Anyone who speaks against the Son of Man can be forgiven, but anyone who speaks against the Holy Spirit will never be forgiven, either in this world or in the world to come.
> —MATTHEW 12:31–32, NLT

So the Holy Spirit is greater here than the Son and the Father. Right now the Holy Spirit is subordinate also to do the ministry of the Son, yet He is not less than the Son or the Father. The Father sent the Son, and the Son sent the Holy Spirit. The Son and the Father cannot do anything without the Holy Spirit. The Son was not incarnated or born without the Holy Spirit. The Son did not say anything without the voice of the Holy Spirit. The Son did not do any miracles or healings without the Holy Spirit. The Father did not create anything in heaven or on earth without the Holy Spirit. And the same Holy Spirit is now living in born-again believers to empower and lead them for their complete assurance to enter into heaven. Still yet the Holy Spirit subordinates Himself to live within the bodies of humans who are born again to create them like Jesus, the Son of God.

When Jesus offered the final sacrifice on the cross to wash the sins of the world, He became greater than the Father and the Holy Spirit, because the Father and the Holy Spirit cannot wash the sins of the world/human beings without Jesus, His holy blood to make relationship with the holy human beings.

Jesus also talked, walked, ate, and slept like humans. He was 100 percent human and He practiced his human nature. He was 100 percent God and He practiced His godly nature too.

Caution: There are some people (not Christian at all) who try to use the human nature of Jesus to prove that Jesus is not God.

IF JESUS WAS GOD THEN WHY WAS HE DEAD ON THE CROSS?

We should know carefully what actually happened when Jesus was on the cross. At the time, Jesus had two natures—one was human (100 percent) and another was God (100 percent)—but while the human Jesus was dead for sinners (according to the human eyes), the Spirit of God (God Jesus) departed from the body of Jesus and went to paradise with the human soul of Jesus to proclaim the gospel to people in paradise that their sin's price He had just paid.

When the human portion of Jesus died, the God Jesus took the human soul of Jesus to paradise to share the good news to the people who lived in paradise that their postpaid bill for their sins was paid by the final sacrifice of Jesus (1 Pet. 3:19–21). And God Jesus (the Spirit) and the human soul of Jesus came back to His body on the third day and He resurrected, lived another forty days with His disciples and true followers, and then ascended to heaven in front of all of them. Then within ten days He sent the Holy Spirit upon them who became holy by receiving the final sacrifice to live with God forever.

So God Jesus did not die, just left the body for three days. God cannot die because He is eternal. The Holy One cannot die because He is the Holy One; that's why Jesus resurrected. But because the sins of the world were upon Him for a short period of time when He was on the cross, Jesus needed to give His blood and left His body to make the final sacrifice for the sinners to make them holy in order to install the Spirit of God (Seed of God) within them. Everyone who is washed by the blood of Jesus automatically receives the Holy Spirit in them because the Holy Spirit is seeking the holy people to live in them. When God breathed into Adam's nostrils the breath of life (Gen. 2:7), Adam received not only life, but the Holy Spirit as an image, likeness of God. And when Adam and Eve disobeyed God, the Holy Spirit (Spirit of God) left them and they were dead spiritually. Jesus came to give us the same Spirit of God in those who believe Him as He is (John 6:27–29; 100 percent human and 100 percent God) to live forever.

First, He made a final sacrifice to wash our sins to make His believers holy (the water); and secondly, He went to heaven and sent the Holy Spirit to fill the holy ones (believers already washed by the blood of Jesus) with the Holy Spirit. So we become spiritually alive to walk with God forever. We will learn more about this in the remaining chapters of this book.

4

LAW VS. FAITH IN CHRIST

N o one was able to become holy, including Abraham, by *law*. Abraham became holy by *faith* (post-paid action, but paid by Jesus alone). How?

> For what does the Scripture say? "Abraham believed God, and it was accounted to him for righteousness."
> —Romans 4:3

> But now the righteousness of God apart from the law is revealed, being witnessed by the Law and the Prophets, even the righteousness of God, through faith in Jesus Christ, to all and on all who believe. For there is no difference; for all have sinned and fall short of the glory of God, being justified freely by His grace through the redemption that is in Christ Jesus, whom God set forth as a propitiation by His blood, through faith, to demonstrate His righteousness, because in His forbearance God had passed over the sins that were previously committed, to demonstrate at the present time His righteousness, that He might be just and the justifier of the one who has faith in Jesus. Where is boasting then? It is excluded. By what law? Of works? No, but by the law of faith. Therefore we conclude that a man is justified by faith apart from the deeds of the law.
> —Romans 3:21–28

Summary: Law cannot save anyone, but can send everyone to hell. We need to live with Jesus by our own faith that leads us to love Him and become like Him.

5

THE LOVE AND GRACE OF GOD ARE ONLY FOUND IN JESUS CHRIST

'But we believe that through the grace of the Lord Jesus Christ we shall be saved in the same manner as they.
—ACTS 15:11

SOME PEOPLE CAN find difficulties with two words, *love* and *grace*. Christ is the love of God for us to save us from sin and hell. We don't have any other choice or way to find the love and grace of God without Christ; that is why Jesus Christ became the way, the truth, and the life to meet with God (John 14:6). *God's love for us is found in Christ alone* (John 3:16).

> Now hope does not disappoint, because the love of God has been poured out in our hearts by the Holy Spirit who was given to us. For when we were still without strength, in due time Christ died for the ungodly. For scarcely for a righteous man will one die; yet perhaps for a good man someone would even dare to die. But God demonstrates His own love toward us, in that while we were still sinners, Christ died for us.
> —ROMANS 5:5–8

When human beings fell and separated from God, they needed grace to restore their holiness and truth to walk with God. "Grace is the first ingredient necessary for growing up in the image of God. Grace is unbroken, uninterrupted, unearned, accepting relationship. It is a kind of relationship humanity had with God in the Garden of Eden."[1] Only Jesus has the grace, truth, and love to make us holy to restore our relationship with God forever.

Summary: The love and the grace of God are *only found* in Jesus and His Spirit, the Holy Spirit.

6
LOVE VS. LAW

D ID GOD EVER say, "I give the world/you law, therefore I send My Son"? Never. But John 3:16 says that
because He loved us/the world so much that He sent His
beloved Son to die for us. Is there any law to receive Jesus
as He is? None. Because, "For Christ is the end of the law
for righteousness to everyone who believes" (Rom. 10:4).
Law cannot make anyone holy, but can send everyone
directly to hell. Jesus came to save us from sin/law, and
recreate us by the Holy Spirit, and will come again to take
us with Him to heaven, not to send us into hell. So whoever is living under the law cannot know the love of God
that is found in Christ to enter into heaven. Law is the
opposite of love as hell is the opposite of heaven. It is true
that Jesus fulfilled the law for us by giving His life for us
on the cross in order to fill us with His Spirit so that we
can live with God forever with love without any law. By
the *love* of God, Christ defeated the law by His death. So,
in the age of the church of Jesus, law has no power over
the love of God, Christ. Now we need to choose only one
Jesus (New Testament Jesus), the love of God or the law.
If we choose law we choose to enter into hell. But if we do
choose love (Jesus) we choose heaven to live with the love
of God forever without any law.

Lucifer became Satan because he wanted to become
like God. He inspired the first humans to become like
God where they ate the forbidden fruit to become like
God, but they became spiritually dead (lost holiness, the
Holy Spirit/the Spirit of God). Then God gave humans

laws to obey those laws to become like God as they desired. Actually, God gave a challenge to humans to become like Him. People of the Old Testament received the challenge to become like God, but failed 100 percent— that we can see clearly. Actually, laws reveal the holiness of God, but trying to obey those laws is a wrong motive. Believers who want to do self-improvement by obeying the Law of the Old Testament are still living in the Old Testament time with the Old Covenant. Old Testament people were not able to obey the law, but punished themselves by the law and lived like slaves of the law; even God gave them those laws. God gave them those laws and told them that He is holy and they must become holy as He is, to become like Him. God gave them law, because humans wanted to become God by obeying the serpent in the Garden of Eden. Still, the fallen human beings have the same motivation in their flesh and mind to become like God. In the Old Testament time, God gave them the law to reveal His attributes to them and give them a challenge to become like Him by obeying those laws. And humans tried and failed. Finally, God became Man (Jesus) because He loved us to make us His children. We need the love of God, Jesus, so we can become holy and empowered by the Holy Spirit to remain holy as the children of God, but not as *the* God.

We can see in details that no one was able to obey the law—even Moses—without Jesus; no human can obey the law. That means all human beings are ready to be punished by the law that they have been trying to obey since the law was given to humanity. But now if we do live by the Holy Spirit we are not under the law, but we are driven by His Spirit to live with love, holiness, peace, sound health, and blessings to worship God forever. We should understand that love principles and regulations are not laws, because the love of God (Jesus in *us*) loves to follow that without making them any law as burden. Why does a born-again person follow the principles of love? Because a born-again person is filled with the Holy Spirit and empowered by the Holy Spirit to exercise the principles of love. The principles of love are the attributes of God that we found in the New Testament as the fruit of the Holy Spirit (Gal. 5:22–23). Actually the fruit of the Holy Spirit are the true characteristics of a born-again person, because he is driven by the Holy Spirit to build God's kingdom. A born-again person does not have any burden of any law, because he is not only having the fruit of the Holy Spirit, or even doing it, but he is also being the fruit of the Holy Spirit.

That's why Jesus gave us brand-new church with the Holy Spirit instead of sending us to the synagogue. If you choose the church then you are under the love of God, but if you choose the law then you are under law and may join any synagogue. The choice is yours. Just know that the characters of love are much better than the law.

One example: Law forces us to disobey God, where love helps us to obey God by the power of the Holy Spirit. Law has no power of the Holy Spirit. Law never makes anyone holy, so whoever is under the law has never had the power of the Holy Spirit to live in the holy place where Jesus lives. What is your choice—love or law? Decide today.

Our faith is not only feelings, but also our own decision to love God and become one with Him through His love and the grace that is only found in Jesus Christ. Jesus is the perfect love of God for us who can make us holy like Him through His holy blood and give us His own Spirit in us to live with Him and for Him forever as children of God. Dr. Billy Graham said in his big gathering in 1979 that we cannot make law to love people, love must need to come from one's heart.[1] That's why everyone needs to be born again, to create a new heart to be filled with the love of God to love one another as we love ourselves and as God loves us through Jesus.

> We were held prisoners by the law.
> —GALATIANS 3:23, NIV

> For if you are trying to make yourselves right with God by keeping the law, you have been cut off from Christ! You have fallen away from God's grace.
> —GALATIANS 5:4, NLT

Law kills love, forces us to commit sins.

> Now hope does not disappoint, because the love of God has been poured out in our hearts by the Holy Spirit who was given to us.
> —ROMANS 5:5

The Holy Spirit has been poured out in our hearts through *love*, not by any *law*.

7
GOD IS NOT LAW, BUT LOVE

Beloved, let us love one another, for love is of God; and everyone who loves is born of God and knows God. He who does not love does not know God, for God is love. In this the love of God was manifested toward us, that God has sent His only begotten Son into the world, that we might live through Him. In this is love, not that we loved God, but that He loved us and sent His Son to be the propitiation for our sins. Beloved, if God so loved us, we also ought to love one another. No one has seen God at any time. If we love one another, God abides in us, and His love has been perfected in us. By this we know that we abide in Him, and He in us, because He has given us of His Spirit. And we have seen and testify that the Father has sent the Son as Savior of the world. Whoever confesses that Jesus is the Son of God, God abides in him, and he in God. And we have known and believed the love that God has for us. God is love, and he who abides in love abides in God, and God in him. Love has been perfected among us in this: that we may have boldness in the day of judgment; because as He is, so are we in this world. There is no fear in love; but perfect love casts out fear, because fear involves torment. But he who fears has not been made perfect in love. We love Him because He first loved us.
—1 JOHN 4:7–19

For God so loved the world that He gave His only begotten Son, that whoever believes in Him should not perish but have everlasting life. For God did not send His Son into the world to condemn the world, but that the world through Him might be saved. He who believes in Him is not condemned; but he who does not believe is condemned already, because he has not believed in the name of the only begotten Son of God. And this is the condemnation, that the light has come into the world, and men loved darkness rather than light, because their deeds were evil. For everyone practicing evil hates the light and does not come to the light, lest his deeds should be exposed. But he who does the truth comes to the light, that his deeds may be clearly seen, that they have been done in God.
—JOHN 3:16–21

THE PRINCIPLE OF love is many times better than law. The law says, "Don't kill"; but love never attempts or gives thought to kill. The law says, "Do not lie"; but love never lies. The law says, "Don't steal"; but love never steals. The law says, "Don't give false witness"; but love never ever gives false witness. That's why there is no law that can go against love. Love kills the law and covers all sins. So we need to know the power of love by practicing only that love found in Jesus Christ.

Why was the Old Covenant with the law?

> For God has imprisoned everyone in disobedience so he could have mercy on everyone.
> —ROMANS 11:32, NLT

Romans 11:32 gives us a crystal-clear, high-definition picture of how the old picture has changed through Jesus. Jesus came as a love of God to live among us to set us free from the slavery of laws. He first gave His blood to wash our sins and then filled us with His Spirit to create us as children of God. When we are able to receive the Spirit of Jesus we surely become children of God to live like Jesus. Jesus was born by the Holy Spirit and filled by the Holy Spirit to live among us as the true Son of God. So the followers of Jesus must need to be born by the Holy Spirit and filled with the Holy Spirit to live like Jesus.

Summary: God will judge us at the final judgment by the principles of *love*, not by any law. That's why our salvation is through love alone, Jesus Christ.

8
WHAT IS THE NEW COVENANT?

From his abundance we have all received one
gracious blessing after another. For the law
was given through Moses, but God's unfailing
love and faithfulness came through Jesus
Christ. No one has ever seen God. But the
unique One, who is himself God, is near to the
Father's heart. He has revealed God to us.
—JOHN 1:16–18, NLT

J ESUS HIMSELF IS God's mercy, grace, and love for us, but not any law, or even force. As human beings we cannot live like God as Lucifer had tried and failed, as Adam and Eve were cheated to become like God and failed, as people in the Old Testament failed by trying to become holy like God under the law, but God came to live with us and in us through Jesus, the New Covenant. So Jesus Himself is the New Covenant living in us to make us the children of God. When we truly become born-again believers we are truly His children.

We just need to follow Jesus to become born-again believers. But if we try to add anything with the New Covenant, Jesus, we completely miss becoming born again to live as children of God. So, the New Covenant ended the Old Covenant because the New Covenant fulfilled the Old Covenant that was done with Abraham, Moses, and David.

For Christ is the end of the law for righteousness to
everyone who believes.

—ROMANS 10:4

THE GLORY OF THE NEW COVENANT

Through the Old Testament law people can say, "We can
do this or obey the law to become like God," as Lucifer
did, and Adam and Eve followed him to separate from
God. In the New Testament, through the New Covenant
God came down, cleaned His chosen ones, and came
inside of them to lead them as children of God. It is God
who is living in them to show the glory of the Lord that
is better than any Old Testament law.

If anyone repents and surrenders to God instead of
saying, "I can live like God by following the laws of God,"
then God can clean him/her by the blood of Jesus in
order to come inside of him/her as a form of the Holy
Spirit to live forever in him/her. But whoever wants to
follow the order "I can do" cannot surrender to Jesus, as
many super-religious Jews were not able to receive Jesus
at the time of primary church. There are still many Jews
who are facing the same theory to live like Jews, not as
children of God by the born-again experience by the
indwelling presence of the Holy Spirit in their lives.

> Do we begin again to commend ourselves? Or do we
> need, as some others, epistles of commendation to
> you or letters of commendation from you? You are
> our epistle written in our hearts, known and read by
> all men; clearly you are an epistle of Christ, minis-
> tered by us, written not with ink but by the Spirit of
> the living God, not on tablets of stone but on tablets
> of flesh, that is, of the heart.
>
> And we have such trust through Christ toward
> God. Not that we are sufficient of ourselves to think of
> anything as being from ourselves, but our sufficiency

is from God, who also made us sufficient as ministers of the new covenant, not of the letter but of the Spirit; for the letter kills, but the Spirit gives life.

But if the ministry of death, written and engraved on stones, was glorious, so that the children of Israel could not look steadily at the face of Moses because of the glory of his countenance, which glory was passing away, how will the ministry of the Spirit not be more glorious? For if the ministry of condemnation had glory, the ministry of righteousness exceeds much more in glory. For even what was made glorious had no glory in this respect, because of the glory that excels. For if what is passing away was glorious, what remains is much more glorious.

Therefore, since we have such hope, we use great boldness of speech— unlike Moses, who put a veil over his face so that the children of Israel could not look steadily at the end of what was passing away. But their minds were blinded. For until this day the same veil remains unlifted in the reading of the Old Testament, because the veil is taken away in Christ. But even to this day, when Moses is read, a veil lies on their heart. Nevertheless when one turns to the Lord, the veil is taken away. Now the Lord is the Spirit; and where the Spirit of the Lord is, there is liberty. But we all, with unveiled face, beholding as in a mirror the glory of the Lord, are being transformed into the same image from glory to glory, just as by the Spirit of the Lord.

—2 CORINTHIANS 3

The New Covenant ended the Old Covenant. You believe it, or not: *truth* is always *true*.

When Jesus died on the cross two things happened: 1. The Old Covenant ended (the covenant made with Abraham, renewed with Moses, and promised to David); and 2. The New Covenant started only through Jesus and His Spirit, the Holy Spirit. The pre-existent Yeshua, Yahweh/Lord made the Old Covenant, and when He died the Old Covenant was fulfilled and ended. And as He promised through the Old Covenant and through His prophets, especially through Jeremiah (31:31–34), Jesus became the New Covenant through His own blood of His death. So until He died, the New Covenant did not exist. Also, when He died the Old Covenant died/ended forever. Then the Old Covenant became a history to know how the New Covenant came to end the Old Covenant. The people in the Old Testament were lost because of the burden of the legal codes of the Old Covenant as a way to welcome the New Covenant (Rom. 11:32). Can a wise man still want to keep the Old Covenant? The people were lost under the Old Covenant; that's why Yahweh was incarnated as Yeshua, to become New Covenant to save us from Old Covenant and from our sin forever to be filled with the indwelling Holy Spirit to empower us to live like God's children.

Now if you want to keep the Old Covenant (even the Old Testament people were not able to keep it—none of them, except Jesus) you cannot get the New Covenant; you cannot wash your sin through the blood of Jesus to be filled with the Holy Spirit. The Old Covenant keepers (even the high priest) were not washed by the blood of Jesus; then, it was not a question for them to be filled with the Holy Spirit. The Old Covenant lovers still have the same problem. That's why they maybe love Jesus, but do not love to be filled with the Holy Spirit because they hate the tongues of the Holy Spirit as an initial proof of being filled with the Holy Spirit. The New Covenant did not have legal codes like the old one, because the indwelling Holy Spirit became the code of the New Covenant in the heart of the people as God told in Jeremiah 31:33. Praise

God day and night to have the New Covenant to live with God perfectly by the indwelling Holy Spirit without old life or even Old Covenant.

> For sin shall not have dominion over you, for you are not under law but under grace.
>
> —ROMANS 6:14, NKJV

9
What Is the Work of God That We Must Do?

"Do not labor for the food which perishes, but
for the food which endures to everlasting life,
which the Son of Man will give you, because
God the Father has set His seal on Him." Then
they said to Him, "What shall we do, that we
may work the works of God?" Jesus answered
and said to them, "This is the work of God,
that you believe in Him whom He sent."
—JOHN 6:27–29

WE WILL ONLY do the work that is love, God's love
for us—Jesus Christ. All our labor is for our love,
who is Jesus Christ alone.

What we must need to believe to come closer to the
Life-giver: *Our salvation is limited to Jesus only.*

> Nor is there salvation in any other, for there is no
> other name under heaven given among men by which
> we must be saved.
>
> —ACTS 4:12

> Then he called for a light, ran in, and fell down trem-
> bling before Paul and Silas. And he brought them out
> and said, "Sirs, what must I do to be saved?" So they
> said, *"Believe on the Lord Jesus Christ, and you will*
> *be saved, you and your household."* Then they spoke
> the word of the Lord to him and to all who were in
> his house. And he took them the same hour of the
> night and washed their stripes. And immediately he
> and all his family were baptized.
>
> —ACTS 16:29–33, EMPHASIS ADDED

"I tell you the truth, those who listen to my message
and believe in God who sent me have eternal life.
They will never be condemned for their sins, but they
have already passed from death into life."

—JOHN 5:24, NLT

"For God loved the world so much that he gave his
one and only Son, so that everyone who believes in
him will not perish but have eternal life. God sent his
Son into the world not to judge the world, but to save
the world through him. There is no judgment against
anyone who believes in him. But anyone who does
not believe in him has already been judged for not
believing in God's one and only Son. And the judgment is based on this fact: God's light came into the
world, but people loved the darkness more than the
light, for their actions were evil. All who do evil hate
the light and refuse to go near it for fear their sins
will be exposed. But those who do what is right come
to the light so others can see that they are doing what
God wants."

—JOHN 3:16–21, NLT

And what do you benefit if you gain the whole world
but are yourself lost or destroyed?

—LUKE 9:25, NLT

If you confess with your mouth the Lord Jesus and
believe in your heart that God has raised Him from
the dead, you will be saved. For with the heart one
believes unto righteousness, and with the mouth con-
fession is made unto salvation. For the Scripture says,
"Whoever believes on Him [Jesus] will not be put to
shame."

—ROMANS 10:9–11

And he told us how he had seen an angel standing in
his house, who said to him, "Send men to Joppa, and
call for Simon whose surname is Peter, who will tell

you words by which you and all your household will be saved."

—Acts 11:13–14

Later Peter told them about Jesus, how He saved them so they were washed by the blood of Jesus and baptized with the Holy Spirit with the evidence of the tongues of the Spirit.

Jesus told him, "I am the way, the truth, and the life. No one can come to the Father except through me."

—John 14:6, nlt

Jesus always said that if you love Me, follow My commands. Jesus only commands us to do three things:

1. Love your God with all your heart, mind, and strength.

2. Love your neighbors as you love yourself.

3. Go, preach, baptize (who believe), make disciples and teach them what I taught you to obey (Matt. 22:36–40, 28:19).

Jesus requested us to "Build up My church."

10

THE SUPREME DECLARATION OF THE VISIBLE GOD, JESUS CHRIST

Jesus answered and said to him, "Most assur-
edly, I say to you, unless one is born again, he
cannot see the kingdom of God." Nicodemus said
to Him, "How can a man be born when he is
old? Can he enter a second time into his mother's
womb and be born?" Jesus answered, "Most assur-
edly, I say to you, unless one is born of water and
the Spirit, he cannot enter the kingdom of God."
—JOHN 3:3–5

A S WE UNDERSTAND from the first chapter that the term "born again" also means "born from above." The substances that we need to be born again are coming from above/heaven. The Water and the Spirit are the two substances that create us as new humans, children of the living God. And these two substances came from heaven. The Water is a metaphor here that is completely none but Jesus alone, because Jesus only came from above/heaven (John 3:13, 8:23–24). The water (H_2O) is the created substance on earth that does not come from heaven. Jesus is God who can only create us to be born again.

What is a metaphor? A metaphor is used to extend our way of thinking to blend/melt the truth to give us a perfect sense of true understanding that helps us to know and remember the truth.

In John 3:5, "the Spirit" is the Holy Spirit who came down from heaven on the Day of Pentecost, that event we can find in Acts 2. In Acts chapter 1, Jesus talked about the Holy Spirit that He is going to send to recreate us and empower us. Now we are going to learn details about the Water and the Spirit to be born again.

How can you receive the New Covenant to be born again as Jesus said in John 3:3, 5?

1. Forget the Old Covenant and all its legal codes, and start to believe Jesus only, who is the New Covenant, where the Holy Spirit is the legal code of the New Covenant. Just worship Jesus and live by the Holy Spirit. There is no law against the Holy Spirit.

2. Repent and confess all your sins to receive Jesus as your Lord, Savior, and King by washing all your sins through His blood.

3. Receive the fullness of the Holy Spirit (be filled with the Holy Spirit) to be born again to enter into heaven (John 3:3, 5).

4. Live with confidence through the power and help of the indwelling Holy Spirit (continuous love counseling to spend every moment of your life). Now the Lord/Yahweh is the Spirit and wherever is the Spirit of the Lord there is complete freedom (2 Cor. 3:17). Enjoy your freedom in the presence and power of the Holy Spirit with righteousness, peace, and joy (Rom. 18:17).

Yes, from here now we will start to know how we can personally apply the New Covenant, Jesus, to be born again to enter into heaven.

Jesus the Man had flesh, blood, human soul, and the

Spirit who is the Holy Spirit, the Spirit of God. So Jesus was 100 percent human and 100 percent God.

THE WATER IS JESUS HIMSELF (JOHN 3:3–5)

The Water, Jesus, came down from above/heaven to give us birth to be born again.

The Water that gives us everlasting life

Jesus is the Living Water (John 4:10). Only Jesus has the Water (substance) that can give us everlasting life.

> Jesus answered and said to her, "Whoever drinks of this water will thirst again, but whoever drinks of the water that I shall give him will never thirst. But the water that I shall give him will become in him a fountain of water springing up into everlasting life."
>
> —JOHN 4:13–14

Jesus came from heaven to give us new birth. In John 3:13, Jesus says, "No one has ever gone to heaven and returned. But the Son of Man (Jesus) has come down from heaven" (NLT). In John 4:10–14, Jesus talked about the "Living Water," that whoever drinks will never thirst and become a fountain of water springing up into everlasting life.

Only God can create us new, because He is the only Creator, and He is our only visible God Jesus; nothing was created without Him (John 1:3), and nothing will be created without Him. Jesus is the only one person who came down from heaven as Water to wash all our sins and went to heaven to pour out His Spirit, the Holy Spirit, for our spiritual birth. This is how we can become born-again believers to enter into heaven. And when we become born again, at that moment we become children of God to inherit His kingdom on earth and in heaven.

Jesus said, "Most assuredly, I say to you, he who hears

My word and believes in Him who sent Me has everlasting life, and shall not come into judgment, but has
passed from death into life" (John 5:24).

Example: the water that Moses gave to the Israelites in
the desert and saved the lives of the children of Israel.

The Living Water is Jesus, not H_2O

Jesus is the only substance (God) by whom we can be
saved, not water (H_2O). The Old Testament always says,
"Who can save us? Only God." Is water (H_2O) God? So
the Water that Jesus talked about here in John 3:3–5 is
Jesus Himself. Jesus always talked with symbols, meta-
phors, and stories. Water baptism is an act of obedience
for us for public declaration of our faith in Jesus, like a
marriage ceremony. Our faith and acts of obedience are
helpful, but salvation is the gift from the Father from
above/heaven. And Heavenly Father's only gift for us is
Jesus Christ for our new birth/salvation/eternal life (John
3:16).

Jesus said: I am Divine (Eternal), I am Good Shepherd,
the Gate/Door of Heaven, Breath of Life, the Bread, the
Cornerstone, the Way, the Truth, the Savior, the Life, the
Living Water.

The Water that heals and restores us for eternal life

Jesus, the Living Water, has sacrificed His flesh to
restore us, heal us, and forgive our sins. The flesh of Jesus
made the final sacrifice for us. The Flesh of Jesus was
blameless, sinless, pure, holy, and perfect for making a
perfect and holy sacrifice to heal us, restore us, and to
forgive our sins. Jesus took thirty-nine stripes/wounds
into His flesh to heal us and restore us completely as a
whole body.

> But He was wounded for our transgressions, He
> was bruised for our iniquities; the chastisement for

our peace was upon Him, and by His stripes we are healed. All we like sheep have gone astray; we have turned, every one, to his own way; And the LORD has laid on Him the iniquity of us all.

—ISAIAH 53:5–6

Who Himself bore our sins in His own body on the tree, that we, having died to sins, might live for righteousness—by whose stripes you were healed.

—1 PETER 2:24

Example: the bread and the blameless meat of the lamb that the children of Israel ate (and posted the blood of the lamb on their doorposts) at the first Passover to save them from the judgment of God in the land of Egypt.

Jesus, the Living Water has sacrificed His 100 percent human soul to give us life, through whom our own soul is saved.

For the life of the flesh is in the blood, and I have given it to you upon the altar to make atonement for your souls; for it is the blood that makes atonement for the soul.

—LEVITICUS 17:11

Surely He has borne our griefs and carried our sorrows; yet we esteemed Him stricken, smitten by God, and afflicted.

—ISAIAH 53:4

Jesus, the Living Water has sacrificed His blood to wash all our sins (original sin, sin-against sins, and personal sins)

And according to the law almost all things are purified with blood, and without shedding of blood there is no remission.

—HEBREWS 9:22

Not with the blood of goats and calves, but with His
[Jesus's] own blood He entered the Most Holy Place
once for all, having obtained eternal redemption.

—Hebrews 9:12

Jesus Christ, the faithful witness, the firstborn from
the dead, and the ruler over the kings of the earth. To
Him who loved us and washed us from our sins in
His own blood.

—Revelation 1:5

And they overcame him [Satan] by the blood of the
Lamb [Jesus] and by the word of their testimony
[believe in Jesus], and they did not love their lives to
the death.

—Revelation 12:11

But if we walk in the light as He is in the light, we
have fellowship with one another, and the blood of
Jesus Christ His Son cleanses us from all sin. If we
say that we have no sin, we deceive ourselves, and the
truth is not in us. If we confess our sins, He is faithful
and just to forgive us our sins and to cleanse us from
all unrighteousness.

—1 John 1:7–9

In Him we have redemption through His blood, the
forgiveness of sins, according to the riches of His
grace.

—Ephesians 1:7

And by Him to reconcile all things to Himself, by
Him, whether things on earth or things in heaven,
having made peace through the blood of His cross.

—Colossians 1:20

Example: the blood that the children of Israel applied
on the door post on the first Passover day to save themselves from the judgment of God in the land of Egypt
(Exod. 12:13).

Jesus Said, "I AM THE LIVING GOD, The Bread of Life. Your forefathers ate manna in the wilderness and they died. This is the Bread that came down from Heaven, that a man may eat of it and he shall not die. I AM THE LIVING GOD, The Living Bread, who has come down from Heaven, and if a man will eat of this bread, he will live for eternity, and the bread that I shall give is my body that I give for the sake of the life of the world." But the Jews were arguing with one another and saying, "How can this man give us his body to eat?" And Yeshua said to them, "Timeless truth I speak to you: Unless you eat the body of the Son of Man and drink his blood, you have no life in yourselves. But whoever eats of my body and drinks of my blood has eternal life, and I shall raise him in the last day. For my body truly is food, and my blood truly is drink. Whoever eats my body and drinks my blood abides in me and I in him."

—John 6:48–56, abpe

How much more shall the blood of Christ, who through the eternal Spirit offered Himself without spot to God, cleanse your conscience from dead works to serve the living God?

—Hebrews 9:14

The Holy Spirit worked as the Fire to present the final sacrifice to God for our salvation (born again life/new life/eternal life/everlasting life). We could not enter into the present kingdom of God (time of grace and love of God) if Jesus had not made the final sacrifice for us. The Holy Spirit cannot come in us to recreate us for eternal life with God without the merit of the final sacrifice that Jesus made for us on the cross, because the Holy Spirit is completely holy and He cannot come inside of an unholy person. The final sacrifice of Jesus on the cross only can wash and clean the repentant sinners from their sins to make them holy in order to fill them with the Holy Spirit. So by applying the blood of Jesus and baptizing in the Holy Spirit we become born-again believers to inherit His kingdom as His children. Let us praise Jesus day and night for what He has done for us!

The blood of Jesus enables us to receive the Holy Spirit. The blood of Jesus makes us holy not only to meet with God, but also to live with Him forever. Through the blood of Jesus we are not going to live with God, but God is coming as the Holy Spirit to live in us as Immanuel. Hallelujah! And when the Holy Spirit lives in us with proper evidences, we are truly God's children to live with God's attributes (fruit of the Holy Spirit).

> On the last day, that great *day* of the feast, Jesus stood and cried out, saying, "If anyone thirsts, let him come to Me and drink. He who believes in Me, as the Scripture has said, out of his heart will flow rivers of living water." But this He spoke concerning the Spirit, whom those believing in Him would receive; for the Holy Spirit was not yet *given,* because Jesus was not yet glorified.
> —JOHN 7:37–39

THE SPIRIT IS THE SPIRIT OF JESUS (JOHN 3:3–5)

The "Spirit" that Jesus talked about here in John 3:3–5 is the Spirit of Jesus, the Holy Spirit, who is the Spirit of God (Gen. 1:2; 1 Cor. 2:11).

> But you are not in the flesh but in the Spirit, if indeed the Spirit of God dwells in you. Now if anyone does not have the Spirit of Christ, he is not His.
> —ROMANS 8:9

> Of this salvation the prophets have inquired and searched carefully, who prophesied of the grace *that*

would come to you, searching what, or what manner of time, *the Spirit of Christ* who was in them was indicating when He testified beforehand the sufferings of Christ and the glories that would follow. To them it was revealed that, not to themselves, but to us they were ministering the things which now have been reported to you through those who have preached the gospel to you by the Holy Spirit sent from heaven—things which angels desire to look into.

—1 PETER 1:10–12, EMPHASIS ADDED

A Promise for all

[The Lord God Almighty said,] "And it shall come to pass afterward that I will pour out My Spirit on all flesh; your sons and your daughters shall prophesy, your old men shall dream dreams, your young men shall see visions."

—JOEL 2:28

A testimony from John the Baptist

"I indeed baptize you with water unto repentance, but He who is coming after me is mightier than I, whose sandals I am not worthy to carry. He will baptize you with the Holy Spirit and fire. His winnowing fan is in His hand, and He will thoroughly clean out His threshing floor, and gather His wheat into the barn; but He will burn up the chaff with unquenchable fire."

—MATTHEW 3:11–12

The Doctrine of the Holy Spirit

The Holy Spirit is Almighty God (Acts 5:3–4). He is eternal Spirit (Heb. 9:14). He is one member of the Godhead, equal to the Father and the Son. He is the Spirit of God (1 Cor. 2:11). He is the Spirit of the Father (Matt. 10:20). He is the Spirit of Jesus (Rom. 8:9). He is the Spirit of truth, love, grace, wisdom, knowledge, understanding, prophecy, revelation, judgment, and adoption

(John 14:17, 15:26; Heb. 10:29; Isa. 11:2, 4:4; Eph. 1:17; Rev. 19:10; Rom. 8:15). He is absolutely good. He can live every place (holy) at the same time, everywhere on earth and in heaven, even in the throne of God. He can talk. He makes His own decisions with His own will that is exactly like the Son and the Father. He is the power of God at the same time He is a person, not a thing or power only. He is Almighty God, power of the Most High. Nothing was created without Him. Jesus did not do anything without Him; even Jesus was not born without Him. He is the one who incarnated Jesus for us. He resurrected Jesus for us. He is a gift and a promise for us from the Father and the Son to live in us to help us to live according to the will of God (born-again life). When He lives in us He is the seal of our salvation/born-again life (Eph. 1:13–14), which means the complete assurance for each of us to enter into heaven.

This is the Holy Spirit that God breathed into the nostrils of the first man, Adam, to create him in the image and likeness of God (Gen. 2:7, 1:26–27). Jesus also breathed the same Holy Spirit upon us (John 20:22) that the believers received on the day of Pentecost to be born again (Acts 2).

Jesus said that it is better for us that He will go above/ heaven, for the reason that the Holy Spirit can come to live in us from above/heaven. Jesus said, "Nevertheless I tell you the truth. It is to your advantage that I go away; for if I do not go away, the Helper will not come to you; but if I depart, I will send Him to you" (John 16:7).

So until Jesus ascended to heaven the Holy Spirit did not come from heaven to live in us to create us as His children with born-again experience. Ten days after His ascension Jesus sent the Holy Spirit upon His believers who were washed by His blood where everyone (120 people) became born-again Christians. We will learn more about this issue in the evidence chapter.

How can I be born again to enter into heaven?

Though the born-again substances (the Water and the Spirit) come from heaven, we have a good part to be done to become born-again persons. We need to follow two steps to be born again. These are simple but faithful steps to take with complete faith on Jesus (or the Godhead) alone. True faith cannot contain any doubt in our hearts, minds, and emotions. True faith always follows the full truth of God that we found in Christ to be born again through His holy blood and His Spirit, the Holy Spirit.

Born by the Water + Born by the Spirit = Born Again, eligible to live with God on earth and later in heaven, also in the new earth and new heaven.

THE WATER BIRTH

First Step: Born in the Water

How can we be born by (in) the water?

1. Repent by looking at the Cross of Jesus:

> Do you despise the riches of His goodness, forbearance, and longsuffering, not knowing that the goodness of God leads you to repentance?
> —ROMANS 2:4

> "The time is fulfilled, and the kingdom of God is at hand. Repent, and believe in the gospel."
> —MARK 1:15

> "I tell you, no; but unless you repent you will all likewise perish. Or those eighteen on whom the tower in Siloam fell and killed them, do you think that they were worse sinners than all other men who dwelt in

Jerusalem? I tell you, no; but unless you repent you
will all likewise perish."

—Luke 13:3-5

Repent therefore and be converted, that your sins
may be blotted out, so that times of refreshing may
come from the presence of the Lord.

—Acts 3:19

To Him all the prophets witness that, through His
name, whoever believes in Him will receive remission of sins.

—Acts 10:43

Repent therefore of this your wickedness, and pray
God if perhaps the thought of your heart may be forgiven you.

—Acts 8:22

As many as I love, I rebuke and chasten. Therefore be
zealous and repent.

—Revelation 3:19

How?

Our Step

Repent, confess, and turn (big move) to the holy God
(continuous process) to apply the final sacrifice, the holy
blood of Jesus.

Repentance is the conviction of our heart, mind, and
soul that comes from inside of us. It helps to confess all
our sins specifically and measurably. It even touches the
hidden sins and ignorance. It opens us as whole for Jesus
to come and apply His holy blood to wash all our sins
and to forgive us completely.

God's Step (From Above)

Jesus's blood washes all our sins (1 John 1:5-9; 1:1-4
witness of the apostle John). God applies the blood of
Jesus from heaven to wash us from our sins if we truly
repent and confess to turn back to holy God to live the

rest of our life. God removes the record of our sins from the heavenly book. He cleans our heart, mind, soul, flesh, and blood to make us totally holy.

> This is the message which we have heard from Him and declare to you, that God is light and in Him is no darkness at all. If we say that we have fellowship with Him, and walk in darkness, we lie and do not practice the truth. But if we walk in the light as He is in the light, we have fellowship with one another, and the blood of Jesus Christ His Son cleanses us from all sin. If we say that we have no sin, we deceive ourselves, and the truth is not in us. If we confess our sins, He is faithful and just to forgive us our sins and to cleanse us from all unrighteousness.
>
> —1 JOHN 1:5–9

> I appeal to you therefore, brothers [and sisters], by the mercies of God, to present your bodies as a living sacrifice, holy and acceptable to God, which is your spiritual worship.
>
> —ROMANS 12:1, ESV

> Do not let any part of your body become an instrument of evil to serve sin. Instead, give yourselves completely to God, for you were dead, but now you have new life. So use your whole body as an instrument to do what is right for the glory of God.
>
> —ROMANS 6:13, NLT

Repentance is our part by the inspiration of the Holy Spirit. If we do it faithfully, the precious holy blood of Jesus washes all our sins according to His promise. It is the nature of God to wash the sins of repented human beings through Jesus Christ alone. It is 100 percent the will of God to wash us from all our sins if we truly repent and confess our sins, and if we are willing to turn to the Holy God.

> For this is good and acceptable in the sight of God
> our Savior, who desires all men to be saved and to
> come to the knowledge of the truth. For there is one
> God and one Mediator between God and men, the
> Man Christ Jesus, who gave Himself a ransom for all,
> to be testified in due time, for which I was appointed
> a preacher and an apostle—I am speaking the truth
> in Christ and not lying—a teacher of the Gentiles in
> faith and truth.
>
> —1 TIMOTHY 2:3–7

The problem is that human beings cannot easily repent for their sins because of self-pride, because they are living by the inspiration of evil spirits in the kingdom of darkness. Until they decide to come back to the kingdom of light (God) they cannot repent and confess their sins to Jesus. So our decision to be washed from all sins by His blood through our true repentance to live a holy life through the power of the Holy Spirit is very important.

Some Christian leaders say that this step is a baptism in the body of Christ. I agree with them. Our sins are washed by His blood and we are healed by His flesh. Paul says we need to wear our new life or we need to be clothed by Jesus.

Important: We need to dip ourselves into His blood and stay there until He comes and glorifies our bodies to live with Him forever in heaven or later in the new earth. (The Holy Spirit told me this truth personally to share with you all.)

Summary: Repentance means to feel deeply sorry for our sins, confess all our sins, and turn into the kingdom of light/holy God by the inspiration of the Holy Spirit to prepare us for the next step (being born in the Spirit).

> Peter replied, "Each of you must repent of your sins
> and turn to God, and be baptized in the name of

Jesus Christ for the forgiveness of your sins. Then you
will receive the gift of the Holy Spirit."
—Acts 2:38, nlt

Caution: The Jewish culture believes that water birth
happens when a baby is born with water from a mother's
womb. Because in John 3:4 Nicodemus asked Jesus if he
needed to go into his mother's womb a second time to
be born again. Some Christian preachers accept this and
believe that one must be born as a human to be born
again. But they do not understand that Jesus did not talk
about it in John 3:3, 5. As human beings we already are
born, but what Jesus tells in John 3:3, 5 is that we need
to be born again not from water (H_2O) in a mother's
womb, but through Him, the Living Water who came
from heaven (John 3:13, 16). So be careful of false teachings, and don't listen to them who are not yet born-again
believers.

The Spirit Birth

Second Step: Born by (in) the Spirit

This second step is totally dependent on our first step,
because unless we become holy by the washing of the
blood of Jesus we cannot ask God to give us His Holy
Spirit to live in us. The Holy Spirit comes from above
(heaven) to create us as new (born again) only when we
are able to apply the blood of Jesus to become completely
holy and pure.

He is the Spirit by which we are made God's children
(Rom. 8:15).

Who can take the second step?

Peter replied, "Each of you must repent of your sins
and turn to God, and be baptized in the name of
Jesus Christ for the forgiveness of your sins. Then you

will receive the gift of the Holy Spirit. This promise is
to you, and to your children, and even to the Gentiles
"all who have been called by the Lord our God."

—ACTS 2:38–39, NLT

Called means "inspired" by the Holy Spirit where we
already were able to take the first step for the second step
by faith (have it already).

Another word: those who already took the first step
can take the second step by their faith created through
the inspiration of the Holy Spirit.

How can one be born in the Spirit (the Holy Spirit/ Spirit of God/Spirit of Christ)?

When the first step is done faithfully we are holy to
receive the Holy Spirit inside of us to complete the second
step.

It is God who enables us, along with you, to stand
firm for Christ. He has commissioned us, and he has
identified us as his own by placing the Holy Spirit
in our hearts as the first installment that guarantees
everything he has promised us.

—2 CORINTHIANS 1:21–22, NLT

And when you believed in Christ, he identified you
as his own by giving you the Holy Spirit, whom he
promised long ago. The Spirit is God's guarantee that
he will give us the inheritance he promised and that
he has purchased us to be his own people. He did this
so we would praise and glorify him.

—EPHESIANS 1:13–14, NLT

But if anyone does not have the Spirit of Christ, he
does not belong to Him.

—ROMANS 8:9, NAS

By waiting with fasting prayer with others

All of the disciples and lovers of Jesus were waiting in
the Upper Room for the baptism of the Holy Spirit. *They*

waited for ten days and nights, because Jesus told them to wait for the baptism of the Holy Spirit.

> Once when he was eating with them, he commanded them, "Do not leave Jerusalem until the Father sends you the gift he promised, as I told you before. John baptized with water, but in just a few days you will be baptized with the Holy Spirit."
>
> —ACTS 1:4–5, NLT

Receiving the Holy Spirit is not only becoming born-again (recreated) Christians but also being filled with the power, because the Holy Spirit is the power of God Himself.

> "But you will receive power when the Holy Spirit comes upon you. And you will be my witnesses, telling people about me everywhere—in Jerusalem, throughout Judea, in Samaria, and to the ends of the earth."
>
> —ACTS 1:8, NLT

Coming of the Holy Spirit

> When the Day of Pentecost had fully come, they were all with one accord in one place. And suddenly there came a sound from heaven, as of a rushing mighty wind, and it filled the whole house where they were sitting. Then there appeared to them divided tongues, as of fire, and one sat upon each of them. And they were all filled with the Holy Spirit and began to speak with other tongues, as the Spirit gave them utterance.
>
> —ACTS 2:1–4

We also can receive the baptism of the Holy Spirit corporately in a gathering when Jesus is baptizing many believers in the Holy Spirit.

Example: Acts 2:1–4, 120 believers in Jerusalem; and many in Cornelius's home, Acts 10.

By waiting with fasting prayer alone

The 120 believers were waiting with fasting and prayer for ten days to receive the Holy Spirit baptism on the Day of Pentecost. We should follow them to receive the Pentecostal outpouring of the Holy Spirit and the fire of God.

We can ask by faith to receive the Holy Spirit inside of us. Jesus said, "If you then, being evil, know how to give good gifts to your children, how much more will your heavenly Father give the Holy Spirit to those who ask Him!" (Luke 11:13).

Saul became Paul and waited for three days with fasting and prayer to receive the Holy Spirit (Acts 9:9, 17).

By the laying of hands of the apostle(s)

> Then Peter and John laid their hands upon these believers, and they received the Holy Spirit.
>
> —Acts 8:17, nlt

> So Ananias went and found Saul. He laid his hands on him and said, "Brother Saul, the Lord Jesus, who appeared to you on the road, has sent me so that you might regain your sight and be filled with the Holy Spirit."
>
> —Acts 9:17, nlt

> As soon as they heard this, they were baptized in the name of the Lord Jesus. Then when Paul laid his hands on them, the Holy Spirit came on them, and they spoke in other tongues and prophesied. There were about twelve men in all.
>
> —Acts 19:5–7

On March 28, 2012, I was in the Philippines for a healing and revival meeting. After praying for the sick people in a church, God told me to lay hands on those who were hungry to be filled/baptized in His Spirit. I called them, and when I laid hands on them many of them received the baptism of the Holy Spirit and started to speak in other tongues.

Danger: Many believe that believing in Jesus is enough for their salvation. Many believe that receiving Jesus is salvation. Many believe that confessing Jesus as Lord and Savior is their salvation. All of these are helpful thoughts and actions to become born again. But these beliefs are not complete unless someone becomes a truly born-again Christian as Jesus said in John 3:3, 5. *We are in danger unless we are born-again Christians/believers. Just know that a half or partial truth is a complete lie. So be careful and don't try to play with your own life to send yourself directly to hell to burn forever.*

Misinterpretation: Some preachers told (tell) that the baptism of the Holy Spirit is only for receiving power to do some supernatural things like Jesus did, but not for salvation/being born again. They only count salvation by only believing in Jesus, or receiving Jesus as Lord and Savior, or repenting, or even confessing sins. *No one will get confirmation for salvation unless they are born by the Holy Spirit* (when the Holy Spirit comes and lives in him/her). *Many Christians are confused because they received a wrong message about salvation, not the born-again message that Jesus gave us in John 3:3–5.*

Remember, all the 120 believers/lovers of Jesus received the baptism of the Holy Spirit but only a few were commissioned by Jesus (Eph. 4:11, Gift of Jesus) to serve with the power of the Holy Spirit. In Cornelius's house all of them received the Holy Spirit, His power, and spoke in other tongues, but we do not know who served the Lord with power. *But according to the angel who appeared to Cornelius, Peter will tell (do) whatever needs to be done for salvation of his household. The Gentile believers were washed by the blood of Jesus and baptized with the Holy*

Spirit with the initial evidence of the tongues of the Holy Spirit.

Someone can draw a line here that Peter did not or cannot baptize them in the Holy Spirit. It was God's part, and God did. I agree with them, but both parts are from God, washing our sins and baptizing in the Holy Spirit. If we faithfully do our part, God is faithful to do His part. If we are washed by His blood at the same time we can receive the Holy Spirit with evidence. If we don't faithfully do the first step, the second step will never happen to us. That's why many Christians are only believers and followers of Christ without born-again experience.

> And it happened, while Apollos was at Corinth, that Paul, having passed through the upper regions, came to Ephesus. And finding some disciples he said to them, "Did you receive the Holy Spirit when you believed?" So they said to him, "We have not so much as heard whether there is a Holy Spirit." And he said to them, "Into what then were you baptized?" So they said, "Into John's baptism." Then Paul said, "John indeed baptized with a baptism of repentence, saying to the people that they should believe on Him who would come after him, that is, on Christ Jesus." When they heard this, they were baptized in the name of the Lord Jesus. And when Paul had laid hands on them, the Holy Spirit came upon them, and they spoke with tongues and prophesied.
>
> —ACTS 19:1–6

Like them, we need evidence to be born again.

Then Paul said, "John indeed baptized with a baptism of repentance, saying to the people that they should believe on Him who would come after him, that is, on Christ Jesus." When they heard this, they were baptized in the name of the Lord Jesus. And *when Paul had laid hands on them, the Holy Spirit came upon them, and they spoke with tongues and prophesied.*" Like them, we need evidence to be born again.

So we need to be born by the Water, the Man Jesus (His flesh, blood, and soul) and also by the Holy Spirit (the Spirit, the Spirit of Jesus, the Spirit of God) in order to become born-again Christians to live with God forever as His beloved children.

Whoever received the Holy Spirit, the Eternal Spirit, all of them have the eternal life to live with God because the Holy Spirit is the Eternal God.

> How much more shall the blood of Christ, who through the eternal Spirit offered Himself without spot to God, cleanse your conscience from dead works to serve the living God?
>
> —HEBREWS 9:14

Good things for some believers but not for all

When some believers received Jesus as their Lord and Savior, repented for their sins, and confessed all their sins, they were washed by the blood of Jesus immediately, and at the same time they received the Holy Spirit (baptism of the Holy Spirit) to become born-again Christians.

Example:

> "He is the one all the prophets testified about, saying that everyone who believes in him will have their sins forgiven through his name." Even as Peter was saying these things, the Holy Spirit fell upon all who were listening to the message. The Jewish believers who came with *Peter were amazed that the gift of the Holy Spirit had been poured out on the Gentiles, too. For they heard them speaking in other tongues and praising God.* Then Peter asked, "Can anyone object to their being baptized, now that they have received the Holy Spirit just as we did?" So he gave orders for them to be baptized in the name of Jesus Christ.

Afterward Cornelius asked him to stay with them for several days.

—ACTS 10:43–48, NLT, EMPHASIS ADDED

Witness of Peter to Jerusalem

"He told us how an angel had appeared to him in his home and had told him, 'Send messengers to Joppa, and summon a man named Simon Peter. *He will tell you how you and everyone in your household can be saved!' As I began to speak*," Peter continued, "*the Holy Spirit fell on them, just as he fell on us at the beginning* [Beginning of the church of Jesus]. Then I thought of the Lord's words when he said, 'John baptized with water, but you will be baptized with the Holy Spirit.' And since God gave these Gentiles the same gift he gave us when we believed in the Lord Jesus Christ, who was I to stand in God's way?" When the others heard this, they stopped objecting and began praising God. They said, "We can see that God has also given the Gentiles the privilege of repenting of their sins and receiving eternal life."

—ACTS 11:13–18, NLT, EMPHASIS ADDED

Important: We need to dip into His Spirit, the Holy Spirit, and stay there until He comes and glorifies our body to live with Him forever in heaven or later in the new earth. (The Holy Spirit told me this truth personally to share with you all.)

In Acts 1:5, Jesus compared the water baptism with the Spirit baptism. Jesus said, "John indeed baptized in water; but you shall be baptized in the Holy Spirit not many days hence." Before, John said that he was giving baptism into water, but Jesus would give us baptism in the Holy Spirit.

So Jesus is the baptizer and the Holy Spirit is the element in whom we are going to receive Jesus's baptism.

Jesus made it clear that through His baptism we are going to become one body through the one Spirit, the Holy Spirit. This is the outpouring of the Holy Spirit, and after this event we can receive the outpouring of the gifts of the Holy Spirit that we need to drink from the same Spirit (1 Cor. 12:13). So in the Holy Spirit we can be baptized, and after receiving the baptism of the Holy Spirit the gifts of the Holy Spirit (1 Cor. 12:8–11) are given for us to drink.

One can receive the Spirit of Christ only by Spirit baptism. Christ did not give us His Spirit at the time of His death on the cross, or at the time of His resurrection or even ascension, but He sent it only on the Day of Pentecost (Acts 2:1–4). New life starts when Christ lives in us as the Spirit of Christ (Rom. 8:9), because it is no longer our life, but Christ's life. If I baptize a piece of white cloth in a jar of liquid red paint, what will be the color of the piece of cloth? Absolutely red. In the same way, when we are baptized in the Spirit of Christ we become like Christ (in Christ), so it is not us, but Christ who lives in us.

Therefore, all of the believers are right who believe that our new life starts when we receive the Holy Spirit baptism. Actually, the Holy Spirit influences a sinner to believe in Jesus; repent for sin; confess sins specifically; ask forgiveness of sins; receive Jesus as Lord and Savior for washing all of the sinner's sins to make him or her clean, pure, and holy (first step: Water birth) in order to baptize him or her with the Holy Spirit (second step: Spirit birth) with the initial evidence of the tongues of the Holy Spirit. This is the born-again experience. The Holy Spirit influences us to become holy by the blood of Jesus coming inside of us to live forever with us, as Jesus promised that He will never leave us nor forsake us. Only the Holy Spirit baptism unites us in Christ's body (church), because the Spirit of Christ (Rom. 8:9) comes in us to dwell in us by the baptism of the Holy Spirit.

If the disciples of Jesus had received the Holy Spirit in the evening of His resurrection day to become born-again Christians to be part of Jesus's body, they could have become a church on that day, but it did not happen. That's why they needed to wait another fifty days to receive the Holy Spirit to be born again to become the body of Christ to start the church of Jesus. In John 20:22 what Jesus did and said were prophetic, because Jesus told them to wait in Acts 1:4–5, 8, and that was fulfilled on the Day of Pentecost (Acts 2:1–4).

We must remember that Jesus died on the cross on the Jewish Passover Day, and He sent the Holy Spirit on the Jewish Pentecost Day. The Jewish Pentecost Day was the day when the Jews were freed from the slavery of Egypt, and enjoyed their freedom with their new law of God and their new harvest later on in their own land. It is also the celebration of the law of God received by Moses on Mount Sinai. Jewish Passover and Pentecost are the shadow of Jesus that surely guided the events of Jesus in the New Testament. Why did Jesus send the Holy Spirit on the Day of Pentecost? The outpouring of the Holy Spirit ended the law of God that was given to Moses, so we are absolutely free from the law of God to enjoy the love of God with the fullness of His Holy Spirit within us. The shadow of Jewish Pentecost became real Pentecost with the fullness of the Holy Spirit.

> For the Lord is the Spirit, and wherever the Spirit of the Lord is, there is freedom.
>
> —2 Corinthians 3:17, nlt

So the outpouring of the Holy Spirit (Spirit baptism) is the perfect freedom from sin and hell to enjoy our freedom with the fullness of the Holy Spirit to enter into heaven.

Without the blood of Jesus no one can become holy to invite the Holy Spirit to live in him. And without the baptism of the Holy Spirit no one can become born again at all. If the Holy Spirit is not living in you, you are not born again to enter into heaven.

Final Word (bottom line): Just know God is limited to save us from hell through Jesus Christ only. And we need to be born again as Jesus told us in John 3:3, 5—that I already explained in this book. Just know our God has limitations because He is holy. We can only become holy through Jesus Christ, a sinless Man, and His sacrifice that was and is final. His Spirit is given to us as the assurance to enter into heaven to live with Him forever. Amen.

11

WHY ME?

D O YOU KNOW that many people were born in Christian families, but they are not born again? They are not going to enter into heaven with Jesus in His second coming, according to Jesus (John 3:3, 5). Although they called themselves Christians without receiving the Spirit of Christ (Rom. 8:9) inside of them; they will not be resurrected in the first resurrection to meet with Jesus in the middle of the sky to enter into heaven with Him (Rev. 20:4–6; Rom. 8:11; and 1 Thess. 4:16–17).

> And I saw thrones, and they sat on them, and judgment was committed to them. Then I saw the souls of those who had been beheaded for their witness to Jesus and for the word of God, who had not worshiped the beast or his image, and had not received his mark on their foreheads or on their hands. And they lived and reigned with Christ for a thousand years. But the rest of the dead did not live again until the thousand years were finished. This is the first resurrection. Blessed and holy is he who has part in the first resurrection. Over such the second death has no power, but they shall be priests of God and of Christ, and shall reign with Him a thousand years.
>
> —REVELATION 20:4–6

For the Lord Himself will descend from heaven with a shout, with the voice of an archangel, and with the trumpet of God. And the dead in Christ will rise first. Then we who are alive and remain shall be caught up

together with them in the clouds to meet the Lord in
the air. And thus we shall always be with the Lord.

—1 Thessalonians 4:16–17

If you failed to resurrect in the first resurrection you
will be resurrected in the second resurrection to enter
into everlasting hell to live there forever.

And I saw the dead, small and great, standing before
God, and books were opened. And another book
was opened, which is the Book of Life. And the dead
were judged according to their works, by the things
which were written in the books. The sea gave up
the dead who were in it, and Death and Hades deliv-
ered up the dead who were in them [second resur-
rection]. And they were judged, each one according
to his works. Then Death and Hades were cast into
the lake of fire. This is the second death. And anyone
not found written in the Book of Life was cast into
the lake of fire.

—Revelation 20:12–15

12
BE SURE OF YOUR SALVATION

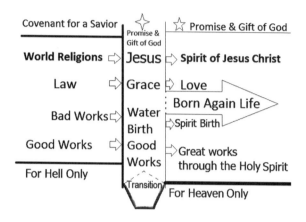

YES, YOU CAN receive complete assurance to enter into heaven.

Again, experience the born-again experience. Eternal life is a promise of God with evidence to those who do not only believe, but also receive His only begotten Son Jesus Christ inside of them as the Spirit of Christ (the Holy Spirit/the Spirit of God; Rom. 8:9; John 3:16). When we receive Jesus Christ inside of us, God installs inside of us the Spirit of Christ as the "complete assurance to enter into heaven" (Gal. 4:4–7; 2 Cor. 1:21–22, 5:5,17; Eph. 1:13–14, Rom. 5:5, 8:9–17; 1 Cor. 6:9–11, 15:42–50).

> It is God who enables us, along with you, to stand firm for Christ. He has commissioned us, and he has identified us as his own by placing the Holy Spirit in our hearts as the first installment that guarantees everything he has promised us.
> —2 CORINTHIANS 1:21–22, NLT

> Now He who has prepared us for this very thing is God, *who also has given us the Spirit as a guarantee.*
> —2 CORINTHIANS 5:5, EMPHASIS ADDED

> In him you also, when you had heard the word of truth,
> the gospel of your salvation, and had believed in him,
> *were marked with the seal of the promised Holy Spirit*;
> this is the pledge of our inheritance toward redemp-
> tion as God's own people, to the praise of his glory.
> —Ephesians 1:13–14, nrsv, emphasis added

The baptism of the Holy Spirit is the seal of our salvation for eternal life to live with God forever.

When the Spirit of Christ comes inside of us we become children of God (1 John 5:1; John 1:12). When we receive the Holy Spirit we become eternal, because the Holy Spirit is eternal. Your two steps (as you learned here) are enough to become eternal sons/daughters of God: 1. Just receive Jesus as He is (His incarnation, life, death, resurrection, ascension, for Water birth); and 2. Receive Him inside of you through the baptism of the Holy Spirit, for Spirit birth (John 3:3–5; Rom. 8:9). Step 1 washes you from all of your sins, and Step 2 happens to you to prove your holiness through Jesus (the Water birth), because the Holy Spirit can only come upon a holy person. If you can receive the Spirit of Christ you will live where He lives after His second coming (John 14:1–3).

Without applying the first step you cannot apply the second step at all. And the second step proves that you already applied the first step, which means if you fail to apply the second step you did not truly apply the first step. *So be careful!*

Just know that eternal life/heavenly life is in Jesus, and when He lives in a person as the form of the Holy Spirit, that person immediately becomes born again to live forever with God. "He who has the Son has life; he who does not have the Son of God does not have life" (1 John 5:12).

Please pray this prayer to be born again if you already repented and confessed all your sins to Jesus. (You need to receive Jesus as your Lord and Savior and repent of your sins and confess them all sincerely before you pray this prayer. This is not a sinner's prayer; it is a repented sinner's prayer).

My Jesus, my Lord and Savior, I love You and I believe that, right now, I am clean and holy through Your precious holy blood. While I am living on earth, I want to live in Your holy way. So I ask You, Lord Jesus, to baptize me in Your Holy Spirit, so I will be able to live in Your holy way. [Please open your heart, to receive the baptism of the Holy Spirit, by faith.]

Dear Holy Spirit, thank You for coming upon me. I am completely convinced that I must live by Your help. Sweet Lord, please help me always to obey You completely and to live in Your holy way. Help me to give witness about this "greatest love of God" to others, by Your power. I want to serve You with my life, time, health, and wealth. Lord, please teach me how to teach others about Your love and love others as well. I want to learn from You, and from Your other children, with a humble spirit. Dear Holy Spirit, please talk with my own spirit and change me as You want. Please speak through me as You wish. Help me to live on earth with love, kindness, joy, and peace, so that I can always pray and worship You. I pray this prayer in the name of my only Lord and Savior, Jesus Christ. Amen."[1]

13
EVIDENCES OF BEING BORN AGAIN TO ENTER INTO HEAVEN

P ROOF OF BORN-AGAIN experience is:

1. Other tongues that are coming through the Holy Spirit who is living in us. It is an utterance from the Holy Spirit as He wishes. He speaks through us directly at the time of need. When the Holy Spirit comes in us He talks through us in His own language that we don't know. We don't even need to learn it. It comes from our heart, not from our brain or mind. Sign is limited by twelve words, but gift is over twelve words to unlimited words. In the Book of Acts, every time believers received the Holy Spirit they spoke with tongues, even the Gentile believers (Acts 2:1–4, 10:44–46, 19:6).

2. Whenever believers receive the Holy Spirit they bear witness about Jesus to all kinds of people through the fire and power of the Holy Spirit (not by human brain only). Jesus declared: "But you will receive power when the Holy Spirit comes upon you. And you will be my witnesses, telling people about me everywhere—in Jerusalem, throughout Judea, in Samaria, and to the ends of the earth" (Acts 1:8).

Just know that whoever has the true other tongues has burden (child-bearing pain) to bear witness to the lost souls to help them to be born again. Actually, the tongues of the Holy Spirit empower us to preach the gospel in the Spirit as Jesus said in Acts 1:8. And without the Holy Spirit we cannot preach the gospel at all to help others become born again. Sure, we can preach by our own brain without the power of the Holy Spirit, but that will not lead others to be born again. But when we are empowered by the Holy Spirit by speaking His tongues, we can help others to be born again by preaching the gospel through the power of the Holy Spirit. Praise the Lord!

THE INITIAL EVIDENCE OF THE SPIRIT BAPTISM

The baptism of the Holy Spirit is a very important experience of Christian life. Many Christians tried to explain the baptism of the Holy Spirit with their own experience or their own understanding of Scriptures, especially from the Book of Acts or history of Christian theology. We understand theoretically, and when we practice we learn it. We learn through our own experiences. There is no assurance that one theory will fit for all people to get the same experience to learn, because every person is unique. Many theologians and denominations gave their own theological theories about the baptism of the Holy Spirit, but when someone is able to experience the baptism of the Holy Spirit personally by following their theological theory, then they finally learn about the baptism of the Holy Spirit. The baptism of the Holy Spirit is the key to receive the Holy Spirit as a gift of the Father and the Son to be driven by the Spirit of Christ for being like Jesus Christ, and speaking in other tongues is the initial evidence of the baptism of the Holy Spirit.

We can only receive the Holy Spirit (as a promise and as a gift) when we are holy by the final sacrifice (that Jesus made on the cross) through the washing of the blood of Jesus. He can come and live in anyone who is holy, forgiven by the final sacrifice, and washed by the blood of Jesus, because He is the most holy God. But He can inspire anyone, even the worst sinner, to repent and receive Jesus as Savior and Lord. When we receive the baptism of the Holy Spirit, at that moment the Holy Spirit comes in us to live with us. And when He comes in us to live within us, He talks through us with His own language that is called other tongues.

Other tongues are the initial evidence of the baptism of the Holy Spirit. When He lives in us we are adopted as children of God. He is the Spirit of adoption. He is like a friend, a best friend. When our best friend is with us, He talks with us according to His will, love, and feelings. If He does not talk with us He cannot become our friend, helper, advocate, or even comforter as Jesus talked about the Holy Spirit. If He cannot talk He cannot show us all the truth or even teach us all the things about Jesus so we can bear witness about Jesus. If He cannot talk through us He cannot empower us to walk with God or to serve Him. If He cannot talk with us He cannot lead us into all the truth.

Jesus also said:

> However, when He, the Spirit of truth, has come, He will guide you into all truth; for He will not speak on His own authority, but whatever He hears He will speak; and He will tell you things to come.
>
> —John 16:13

> But when the Helper comes, whom I shall send to you from the Father, the Spirit of truth who proceeds from the Father, He will testify of Me. And you also

will bear witness, because you have been with Me
from the beginning.

—JOHN 15:26–27

When God lives in us He uses us with His power
in some special ways called the gifts of the Holy Spirit
(1 Cor. 12:8–11). When He lives in us He also produces
fruit that we call the fruit of the Holy Spirit (Gal. 5:22–23).
When the Holy Spirit, the eternal Spirit, lives in us and
talks in us and through us, we are confirmed 100 percent that we have eternal life, which means we are born-
again Christians. He talks in our own spirit that we are
the sons and daughters of God (Rom. 8:16). He praises
God and gives prophecy through our own mouths with
His own languages that we never learned, the evidence/
sign that He is living in us. So tongues of the Holy Spirit
are the initial evidence of the baptism of the Holy Spirit.

THE BOOK OF ACTS

In Acts 2:3–4, the early believers and apostles gathered
in a place that was shaken, and they were filled with the
Holy Spirit. The Holy Spirit came upon them like a tongue
of fire and immediately they started to speak in tongues
that they had never learned. They spoke as the Holy Spirit
gave them utterance. They also received power of the Holy
Spirit to speak the truth of God boldly. It changed their
lifestyle, character, word, and action. They became charismatic by doing signs and wonders through the power of
the Holy Spirit. "The initial Pentecost charism of tongues
was in evidence among these signs and wonders."[1] As
Paul had said, the other tongues is a sign (1 Cor. 14:22)
and also a gift for the Spirit-filled believers (1 Cor. 12:10).

In Acts chapter 8 Philip was filled of the Spirit and
wisdom to go to Samaria to preach the gospel:

> Then Philip went down to the city of Samaria and
> preached Christ to them. And the multitudes with
> one accord heeded the things spoken by Philip,
> hearing and seeing the miracles which he did. For
> unclean spirits, crying with a loud voice, came out of
> many who were possessed; and many who were para-
> lyzed and lame were healed. And there was great joy
> in that city.
>
> —ACTS 8:5–8

The Holy Spirit used Philip to do signs and wonders
among the Samaritans because he was baptized in the
Holy Spirit. And the signs and wonders through the
power of the Holy Spirit helped the Samaritans to receive
Jesus and water baptism in the water. But they did not
receive the baptism of the Holy Spirit until Peter and
John went there to lay hands on them.

Here, we can see that Paul's baptism of the Holy Spirit
is different than others where he did not baptize in the
water in order to receive the baptism of the Holy Spirit.
Paul met with Jesus face-to-face and became blind as
a result of his encounter with the glorified Son of God.
Ananias became a chosen vessel of God to help Paul to
recover his sight and receive the baptism of the Holy
Spirit. He went to Paul and said, "Brother Saul, the Lord
Jesus who appeared to you on the road by which you
came, has sent me that you may regain your sight and be
filled with the Holy Spirit."[2]

Paul was a persecutor of Christians before he met with
Jesus on the way to persecute Christians. His encounter
with the Lord Jesus led him to receive the baptism of the
Holy Spirit in order to become His apostle. Paul said later
on that he spoke with other tongues as a gift of the Holy
Spirit.

In the same manner, in Acts 10, Roman Gentiles

received the baptism of the Holy Spirit before the water baptism. Of course, Paul and these Roman Gentiles took water baptism after receiving the baptism of the Holy Spirit. Cornelius had four qualities, "a devout man and one who feared God with his entire household, who gave alms generously to the people, and prayed to God always" (Acts 10:2).

For this reason the angel of the Lord came to him and said, "Send men to Joppa, and call for Simon whose surname is Peter, who will tell you words by which you and your entire household will be saved" (Acts 11:13–14). When Peter told them about Jesus, that whoever believes in Him will receive forgiveness of sins, the Holy Spirit fell upon all of them who heard the word. So the Gentile believers received the Holy Spirit (baptism of the Holy Spirit) as the apostles received at Pentecost, which means immediately they started to speak in tongues as the Holy Spirit gave them utterance.

The Holy Spirit falls on the Gentiles

While Peter was still speaking these words, the Holy Spirit fell upon all those who heard the word. And those of the circumcision who believed were astonished, as many as came with Peter, because the gift of the Holy Spirit had been poured out on the Gentiles also. For they heard them speak with tongues and magnify God. Then Peter answered, "Can anyone forbid water, that these should not be baptized who have received the Holy Spirit just as we have?" And he commanded them to be baptized in the name of the Lord. Then they asked him to stay a few days" (Acts 10:44–48).

In Ephesus the disciples of John the Baptist needed to be baptized in the name of Jesus in order to receive the baptism of the Holy Spirit to speak in tongues.

> Then Paul said, "John indeed baptized with a baptism
> of repentance, saying to the people that they should
> believe on Him who would come after him, that is, on
> Christ Jesus." When they heard this, they were bap-
> tized in the name of the Lord Jesus. And when Paul
> had laid hands on them, the Holy Spirit came upon
> them, and they spoke with tongues and prophesied.
> —ACTS 19:4–6

John's baptism of repentance is not enough to receive
the baptism of the Holy Spirit, because that does not
help to apply the blood of Jesus to become holy. "One
can scarcely improve on the observation that 'they were
therefore baptized again in a Christian sense, and when
Paul laid his hands on them, they received the Holy Spirit
in Pentecostal fashion.'"[3]

They also receive the proof of their Spirit baptism:
"they spoke with tongues and prophesied" (v. 6). Only the
baptism of the Holy Spirit enabled them to speak with
tongues and give prophecies.

AZUSA STREET MISSION REVIVAL

Here we want to see the theological truth and value of
the Azusa Street Mission Revival that led thousands of
believers to be baptized with the Holy Spirit with the evidence of tongues. What was the main theme or core value
of the teaching of the Azusa Street Mission Revival? Who
received this biblical or theological truth from whom?
Did they practically experience this truth? What did the
believers receive from the Azusa Street Mission Revival?
And finally, what happened to the whole world?

We will find the answers to these questions that will
help to prove my argument here that the tongues of the
Holy Spirit is the initial evidence of the baptism of the
Holy Spirit to become born-again believers.

As we know, the main person of the Azusa Street Mission Revival was William Joseph Seymour. He was the son of former salves, Simon and Phillis. He was born on May 2, 1870, in Centerville, Louisiana.[4] He was the oldest in a large family, and lived his early years in extreme poverty. He was an African American, one-eye-blind, humble man to become the vessel of God as the pioneer of the Pentecostal Revival at the Azusa Street. He grew up as a Baptist, but joined the Methodist meetings and received the holiness teachings when he was in Indianapolis. Seymour joined "God's Bible School" in Cincinnati to understand the holiness theology clearly.

Then, he went to Houston with his spiritual hunger and heard about Charles Fox Parham's new Bible school. At that time black people were not allowed to sit in the classroom with white people, so Parham told Seymour to sit in the hallway to hear his lectures through an open door.[5] Here he received his theological teachings from Parham, and believed that other tongues is the initial biblical evidence of the baptism of the Holy Spirit. He received his teachings in Houston, but did not receive the experience of the baptism of the Holy Spirit with tongues.

Many Houstonians came to join Parham's services and receive the baptism of the Holy Spirit with tongues. Lucy Farrow, who was a maidservant of Parham before, received the baptism of the Holy Spirit with tongues. Actually, Parham's theology of the baptism of the Holy Spirit with tongues was first established from one of his students experience of the Baptism of the Holy Spirit with tongues. His young student Agnes Ozman was baptized in the Holy Spirit with tongues on January 1, 1901.

> A student of former Methodist pastor and holiness teacher Charles Fox Parham, Ozman received

a startling manifestation of the gift of tongues and become, in effect, the first Pentecostal of the 20th century.[6]

It helped Parham to develop his theology of the baptism of the Holy Spirit with the evidence of tongues to teach his students.

Here Seymour received the truth about the baptism of the Holy Spirit with the evidence of tongues, but he was not able to receive it. Even he had spoken about it from a holiness church pulpit.

> When Seymour preached his first sermon at the Holiness Church on Santa Fe Street, he took as his text Acts 2:4 and declared that speaking in tongues was the "Bible" evidence of receiving the Holy Spirit, although he as yet had not received the experience.[7]

It proved his faithfulness to the truth regarding the baptism of the Holy Spirit. Many believers talk against the tongues because they did not receive personally, and actually, that's why they cannot receive tongues as their evidence of the baptism of the Holy Spirit. God sees our heart. So finally Seymour received the baptism of the Holy Spirit with tongues with seven others.

> For several days prayer services continued in the Asbery homes until the night of April 9, 1906, when Seymour seven others fell on the floor in a religious ecstasy, speaking in tongues.[8]

It proved again that when we honor the truth of God as it is, God is faithful to pour out His Spirit in us, who speaks through us to exalt His holy name that is the proof of the baptism of the Holy Spirit to be born again.

Then Seymour came to his Jerusalem to make Pentecostal revival for the world at the Azusa Street. He found a big building to do revival services where many could come and receive the experience of the baptism of the Holy Spirit with the evidence of other tongues. So in Azusa Street Mission Revival, Seymour was the key person to bless many believers to receive the baptism of the Holy Spirit with the evidence of other tongues.

Many people came to this revival from all over America, and most of them received the baptism of the Holy Spirit with the evidence of tongues and went back to their places, or even other nations, to help others to receive the baptism of the Holy Spirit. Many key leaders from holiness movements and churches came to Azusa Street Mission Revival, and received the baptism of the Holy Spirit with the evidence of other tongues.

Everyone who came to the Azusa Street Mission Revival believing the original doctrine of the baptism of the Holy Spirit with the initial evidence of other tongues received the baptism of the Holy Spirit with tongues.

But those who did not believe the original doctrine of the baptism of the Holy Spirit with the initial evidence of other tongues and went against this doctrine and criticized it badly never received the baptism of the Holy Spirit and were never ever able to speak with other tongues. Even some of the holiness church leaders talked against the baptism of the Holy Spirit. Alma White is the number one:

> Calling Seymour and Parham "rulers of spiritual Sodom," White called speaking with other tongues "this satanic gibberish" and the Pentecostal services "the climax of demon worship."[9]

We can see how holy was this holiness leader of the "Pillar of Fire" who was not only against the languages of the Holy Spirit, but also said that the tongues of the Holy Spirit was a satanic work. This is sin against the

Holy Spirit, but she called herself a holiness Christian leader. Jesus explained sin against the Holy Spirit well in Matthew 12:22–37 that if any man talks against the works/action of the Holy Spirit, it counts as a sin against the Holy Spirit.

On the other hand, many holiness pastors and laymen received the doctrine of the baptism of the Holy Spirit with the evidence of other tongues:

> The first white man to receive the experience at Azusa was one A. G. Garr, pastor of a holiness mission in Los Angeles.[10]

Many new Pentecostal groups, movements, churches, and denominations were born out of this Azusa Street Mission Revival:

> It was precisely this settlement, that tongues were 'the' evidence of the reception of the Holy Spirit, that gave Pentecostalism its greatest impetus.[11]

There were many criticisms and divisions that ended the Azusa Street Mission Revival, but in the meantime this revival went far from Azusa Street to where no one could stop it. This revival did not belong to a place, but was in the hearts of believers who had spoken in tongues as proof of their baptism of the Holy Spirit.

Thousands of believers received the baptism of the Holy Spirit with the evidence of other tongues that helped millions of believers to receive the baptism of the Holy Spirit with the evidence of tongues all over the earth. So it proved that tongues is the God-chosen and perfect initial evidence of the baptism of the Holy Spirit to be born again.

THE THEOLOGIANS OF THE TWENTIETH AND TWENTY-FIRST CENTURIES

Dr. Jack Hayford said that tongues are the first physical sign of a person's becoming Spirit-filled. He also said:

> The church was born at Pentecost with the sign upon its lips ("They were all filled with the Holy Spirit and began to speak with other tongues as the Spirit gave them utterance" —Acts 2:4) makes it impossible to consider it insignificant. With his creative resources as God Almighty, he might have designed any one of ten thousand things as indicators or signals of his working on so historic an occasion as the beginning of the church. As it is, he chose "speaking with tongues" as one phenomenon to be included, and considering its recurrence elsewhere in the early church, it cannot be consigned to a "one-time-only" concept.[12]

God is sovereign to select the evidence of the baptism of the Holy Spirit, and He has chosen the tongues of the Holy Spirit as the initial evidence of the baptism of the Holy Spirit. His church was born by the baptism of the Holy Spirit with tongues as a baby born with his/her cry and own languages.

Here, it is clear by Dr. Hayford that God Himself chose the physical evidence of the baptism of the Holy Spirit, and with the same evidence the early Christians built the first church in Jerusalem on Sunday. So speaking in the tongues of the Holy Spirit is the initial evidence of the baptism of the Holy Spirit to become a born-again believer.

It is absolutely true that the evidence and the experience of the baptism of the Holy Spirit need to be practical rather than theoretical. So the great theology is to study about God with evidence and personal experience of the baptism of the Holy Spirit with the initial evidence of tongues.

> The most particular feature of Pentecostalism is the
> close identification of baptism in the Spirit with
> speaking in tongues. By far the largest section of
> Pentecostals believe that speaking in tongues is 'the
> initial (physical) evidence of baptism in the Spirit.[13]

Veli-Matti Kärkkäinen, a European and a theologian
in the Fuller Theological Seminary, actually quoted this
statement from Gary B. McGee's book entitled *Initial
Evidence*. Personal experience is practical; that makes the
things original to us. So other tongues is not only theoretical or historical, but also practical, as we are speaking
today when we are filled with the Holy Spirit.

Here we should also know that speaking in other
tongues is not only the initial evidence of the baptism
of the Holy Spirit, but it is also a gift of the Holy Spirit
that helps us to produce the fruit of the Holy Spirit for
creating us to become like Jesus, to live and serve His
present kingdom.

> Speaking in tongues is God's designed first "initial"
> sign that the Holy Spirit with power has come into a
> person. And speaking in tongues is ONE of the gifts
> of the Spirit: these two have different purposes.[14]

All those who received the baptism of the Holy Spirit
may not receive the gifts of the other tongues, but surely
received the other tongues as initial evidence (sign).

On the other hand, many people have a wrong idea
about the tongues of the Holy Spirit, because they do not
have any experience of the baptism of the Holy Spirit
with the evidence of tongues. And without personal experiences we cannot learn originally about the baptism of
the Holy Spirit. We should not be surprised of the logics/
reasons of those who do not have any experience with

the baptism of the Holy Spirit with the initial evidence of tongues.

One of them is Charles Caldwell Ryrie, who says, "But everything indicates that the need for the gifts has ceased with the production of the written Word. Certainly the standard Pentecostal position that tongues are the necessary accompaniment of the baptism of the Holy Spirit is not valid."[15]

Many also went against the tongues of the Holy Spirit without understanding that they were going against God, the Holy Spirit:

> It isn't the absence of tongues themselves but the absence of the infilling of the Holy Spirit with power that is accompanied by the presence of other tongues as the Spirit gives the utterance.[16]

So actually these people do not miss the tongues, but miss the baptism of the Holy Spirit, because the tongues of the Holy Spirit is the initial evidence of this baptism.

> Of course, I repeat that speaking in tongues in itself is not the fullness of the Holy Spirit, but as confirmed in the Scriptures tongues is the common external sign that a person has received the fullness of the Holy Spirit.[17]

So those who did not eat an apple cannot tell the taste of the apple. Those who already received the baptism of the Holy Spirit agreed that the tongues are the initial evidence of the baptism of the Holy Spirit.

Here we can see the next level of our understanding about the tongues of the Holy Spirit. What is the gift of other tongues? It is words/languages of the Holy Spirit that come through our mouth. We are not speaking it; God who lives in us is speaking these languages through us. It proves that the Spirit of Christ is in us and we are in Christ. It also proves that Christ leads our lives. So it is no longer us who live, but Christ lives in us. It is our new life's languages and future hope of our resurrection in the first resurrection (Rom. 8:11; Rev. 20:4–6).

How can a believer of Jesus ignore the speaking in tongues as the evidence and experience of the baptism of the Holy Spirit? Praise the Lord that most true biblical believers are still speaking in tongues since they received the baptism in the Spirit to grow in Christ. The tongues of the Holy Spirit prove that He lives in us. When He lives in us, He talks to us and through us. And when He talks through us, He creates us to be like Jesus.

Therefore, the sign of the baptism of the Holy Spirit is Jesus Himself, because the word *tongues* is similar to the Word, Jesus (John 1:1, 14; Rev. 19:13). Jesus also declared that "He who believes and is baptized will be saved; but he who does not believe will be condemned. And these signs will follow those who believe: In My name they will cast out demons; they will speak with new tongues" (Mark 16:16–17).

The words *believe, saved, baptism, sign, casting out demons,* and *speaking new tongues* are important to encounter with Jesus personally. But only when the Holy Spirit lives in a person by the baptism of the Holy Spirit with tongues can he or she grow in Christ by the help of the Holy Spirit. So when He lives in us He talks through us with His own languages—the tongues of the Holy Spirit, a perfect God-given initial evidence of the baptism of the Holy Spirit.

Theology is not talking with God, but studying about God to know Him. But when God talks to us we can know Him better without studying about Him. The Holy Spirit baptism is not logic, or even a theology, but a perfect gift of God that He promised to us, and He fulfilled

His promise (Acts 2:16–21). When we are able to receive the baptism of the Holy Spirit like the apostles of Jesus we know that the Holy Spirit is giving us utterance to speak the tongues that we never learned, because He lives in us and praises God with His own words. Therefore, I stand resolved that the baptism of the Holy Spirit is the key to receiving the Holy Spirit as a gift to be driven by the Holy Spirit for being like Jesus, and the new tongues is the initial evidence of the baptism of the Holy Spirit to become born-again believers. If anyone denied the tongues of the Holy Spirit he denied the Holy Spirit; he denied God, the Word of God, salvation, and the baptism of the Holy Spirit to be born by the Spirit to enter into heaven.

My first word for this discussion is that the Holy Spirit is eternal, and if we don't have the Holy Spirit inside of us, it means that we simply don't have the eternal life/ new life/born-again experience. And when the Holy Spirit comes in us to live within us, He immediately talks through us (initial sign: tongues that we never learned) and also He talks to us clearly with our own spirit and says that we are His children (Rom. 8:16).

Then He leads us to bear witness for Jesus to help others to receive the same experiences that we have. When we are driven by the Holy Spirit, we are empowered by the Holy Spirit to serve His present kingdom with His own power. So it is clear to me that without the baptism of the Holy Spirit, the Holy Spirit cannot live in us to create us to become born-again believers.

There are some good evidences

"Born in the water" means born in the Living Water who is Jesus Christ Himself. Jesus used a metaphor to talk about Himself. Believing in Jesus, His incarnation, life, works, sufferings, blood, death, resurrection...all of these help us to be holy if we believe, repent, and confess all our sins to turn 180 degrees to the Holy God from our sinful nature.

This process can be fulfilled through the water baptism as a public declaration of our faith in Jesus, His life, death, and resurrection, as Paul had said. If someone really can do it with his/her own faith, understanding, and action, God is faithful to forgive him/her through Jesus, the Living Water, and then he or she can be filled and baptized in the Holy Spirit (receive the Holy Spirit inside) by faith at the same time (Acts 10, 19, and 8:16). Acts 8:16 is very clear that the believers who believed in Jesus even though they received the water baptism in the name of Jesus did not receive the Holy Spirit: "For as yet He had fallen upon none of them. They had only been baptized in the name of the Lord Jesus" (NKJV). So, until they received the Holy Spirit they did not become born-again believers.

So the born-again experience is only complete when someone is able to receive the baptism of the Holy Spirit/receive the Holy Spirit inside of him or her. (Being baptized and being filled with the Holy Spirit are the same.) The second step to being born again is a proof of the first step, which means if someone did not do the first step he/she cannot do the second step, because the Holy Spirit cannot come to live in an unholy person. Of course, He can inspire anyone to do the first step to being born again. He is just seeking a person who is willing to apply the final sacrifice of Jesus to come in and live in that person (Rev. 3:20).

John Wesley was never confirmed for being born again through his two methods. We don't want to make methods; we just follow Jesus as He said and as He did for us. He cleaned us (made us holy/washed all our sins) to live in us—that was done perfectly after ten days of His ascension on Sunday, the day of the Jewish Pentecostal day.

So whoever doesn't receive the baptism of the Holy Spirit will always live in doubt without any proof of his or her salvation. *We need to remember that being born in the Water and in the Spirit is very important to live in heaven.* Otherwise we will live forever in hell. Who wants to take a hell-sized risk with his or her own life? Personally, I don't.

If water baptism is the act of obedience to receive Jesus for washing all our sins (being born of the water, the Living Water; many theologians call this act as salvation, conversion, even born again or new life), then the baptism of the Holy Spirit is the fulfillment of the promise of the Father and Jesus to be born again completely.

If someone has not yet received the baptism of the Holy Spirit, he or she is not yet washed by the final sacrifice of Jesus and is still living in sin. He has not yet truly repented and turned 180 degrees to the holy God (true surrender to Jesus) to become holy by the blood of Jesus. His heart is different than his word. So, even though he believed in Jesus or received Jesus (by mouth) as Savior and Lord, it doesn't help him to be born again by the Living Water and the Spirit. Just know that a half or partial truth is a complete lie.

> Jesus said to them again, "Peace to you! As the Father has sent Me, I also send you." And when He had said this, He breathed on them, and said to them, "Receive the Holy Spirit."
> —JOHN 20:21–22

Verse 21 is very clear that this act of breathing is the same purpose of Acts 1 and 2. Jesus said as the Father sent Him He sent His disciples (John 20:21); in Acts 1:4 Jesus said wait for the Holy Spirit; and in Acts 1:8, He made it clear how we will bear witness about Him. And as we know, they all received the Holy Spirit in Acts 2:1–4. So what Jesus said in John 20:22 was fulfilled in Acts 2.

> In anticipation of the coming of the Spirit and to certify the fulfillment of that promise, Christ "breathed on them and said, 'Receive the Holy Spirit'" (John 20:22). While the Holy Spirit would not come on them until that event recorded in Acts 2, Christ's breathing on them was a foretaste of what they would experience on that occasion.[18]

So it is very clear that the true believers and followers of Jesus received the baptism of the Holy Spirit on the first day of the church of Jesus. And that's why the church of Jesus was established, because the Holy Spirit made them all as one body of Jesus. And without the baptism of the Holy Spirit no one can become part of the body of Christ, the true church. The church of Jesus is not a human organization, but it is from above through the baptism of the Holy Spirit with born-again experience. The Holy Spirit, the Spirit of Jesus, is the breath (life) of the church, the body of Jesus. This means that without the Holy Spirit the body of Jesus is dead, and without the baptism of the Holy Spirit no one is a true Christian.

Whoever made his or her own theology that John 20:22 is being born again once and for all is living a life without any proof that they are really born again, because they cannot prove that the Holy Spirit is living in them. They just believe. But Jesus did not make us blind believers, but wise believers who built house on the rock, the solid foundation, with proof, because He lives in us and talks through us (His tongues: initial sign of the baptism of the Holy Spirit). Amen.

Another proof

The Scripture in 1 Corinthians 12:3 says, "So I want you to know that no one speaking by the Spirit of God will curse Jesus, and no one can say Jesus is Lord, except by the Holy Spirit" (NLT). Why? I believe it proves that when we are speaking by the Spirit of God, the other tongues that we never learned, the Holy Spirit lives in us and He talks through us. And when He lives in us we cannot talk against the true living God, Jesus.

Our own tongues prove who we are, in the same way the tongues of the Holy Spirit prove His manifestation within us. "I want to reassure you that no Spirit-filled Christian, speaking in tongues as the Spirit of God gives utterance, will ever blaspheme Jesus."[19] Then it raises a simple statement: Anyone who is not a Spirit-filled Christian (speaking in tongues) can curse Jesus, or convert to any world religion to ignore or deny Jesus.

So there is a huge difference between the believer who is a Spirit-filled Christian speaking in tongues, and those who are just Christians and not Spirit-filled, not speaking in tongues.

I believe that speaking in other tongues is very important to grow in Christ. It does not only prove that the Holy Spirit lives in us, but also proves that He is helping to manifest Himself within us to reveal the Father and the Son (John 14:21, 23). The tongues are the direct words of God from the Spirit of God that help to build our lives upon the Living Word, Jesus, because other tongues represent Jesus and glorify Him always.

Without speaking in tongues as the Holy Spirit gives us utterance we cannot worship God in the Spirit. "But the hour is coming, and now is, when the true worshipers will worship the Father in spirit and truth; for the Father is seeking such to worship Him. God is Spirit, and those who worship Him must worship in spirit and truth" (John 4:23–24). The Holy Spirit is the Spirit of truth who can only lead us to worship in truth.

So when we are speaking in tongues we are speaking the truth of God through the Spirit of God. Who knows the heart of God? Only His Spirit:

> But God has revealed them to us through His Spirit. For the Spirit searches all things, yes, the deep things of God. For what man knows the things of a man except the spirit of the man which is in him? Even so no one knows the things of God except the Spirit of God.
> —1 Corinthians 2:10–11

When the Holy Spirit speaks through us, He reveals the truth of God within us, even though we don't understand His words unless He gives us the interpretation in our language. When we speak the tongues of the Holy Spirit, He produces His fruit in us and empowers us with other gifts of the Holy Spirit to produce His fruit where we have the mind of Christ to grow in Christ.

How can we worship God and pray according to the Father's will?

Jesus said:

> "But the hour is coming, and now is, when the true worshipers will worship the Father in spirit and truth; for the Father is seeking such to worship Him. God is Spirit, and those who worship Him must worship in spirit and truth."
> —John 4:23–24

Can anyone worship in spirit and truth without the Holy Spirit and His utterances?

As we know, the Holy Spirit is the Spirit of truth who will lead (empower/tell/speak) us to all truths. Without the baptism of the Holy Spirit and the tongues of the

Holy Spirit it is impossible to worship God in spirit and truth. The tongues of the Holy Spirit are not from the human's brain, but from above (heaven), because the Spirit is from heaven. The tongues of the Holy Spirit truly open our eyes to see the truth to walk in the light of the truth of God. When He talks He enables us to do things for God and to walk with Him.

Caution: The evil spirits are giving other tongues to their followers too. Fifteen years ago I went to a Hindu area, where God used me to heal many people. I was praying in tongues most of the time and when I just touched the sick people they got healed. At the time, I met a Hindu-devoted lady who was very devoted to Hindu gods. When I was praying in front of her with tongues she became angry and told me that her gods gave her other tongues that she did not learn. Then she started to pray in tongues. I continued to speak in tongues in a loud voice, and she ran away to her home to hide. I did not go after her, but left that place to pray for more sick people in different places.

I also found out that some pastors and laymen had only copied or learned their tongues from other people. They are not truly baptized in the Holy Spirit.

Therefore, we need to have both tongues (inside; word) and evangelism (outside; work) to prove that we received the Holy Spirit inside of us and are born again. If we do not receive these two evidences, it proves that our sin is not forgiven yet, and we do not receive the Holy Spirit at all. So both evidences are necessary, with other gifts of the Godhead, to be driven by the Holy Spirit to become like Jesus. Evangelism is an office (Eph. 4:11) with all of the gifts of the Holy Spirit (1 Cor. 12:8–11) and anointing of the Holy Spirit as Jesus said in Luke 4:18–19:

Lord Jesus Christ, who proclaimed, "The Spirit of the Lord is upon Me, because He has anointed Me

1. To preach the Gospel,

He has sent Me

2. To heal the sick,

3. To proclaim liberty to the captives,

4. To set free the oppressed,

5. To proclaim the acceptable year of the Lord" (Luke 4:18–19)

All of these works of the Holy Spirit are proofs of our salvation/born-again experience/new life through the final sacrifice (Jesus) and the Spirit (of Jesus); this means baptism into Jesus's body and soul to receive His Spirit through the baptism of the Holy Spirit. So we need both the *word* (other tongues of the Holy Spirit) and *work* (works of the Holy Spirit; especially evangelism [Acts 1:8]) as our complete assurance of being born again to enter into heaven.

When we receive these two evidences, we finally become part of the body of Christ, the church. Praise the Lord! When we do have both evidences, we are 100 percent confirmed that we are going to enter into heaven to live with God forever and ever. Amen.

14

BECOMING LIKE JESUS

Secret of the Use of the Power of the Holy Spirit

After receiving the baptism of the Holy Spirit, if you give chance to the Holy Spirit to speak through you two hours (at least) every day, you will be able to become loaded with His power to bear witness about Jesus by preaching the gospel of being born again, by healing the sick and doing miracles in Jesus's name. You will be able to cast out the demons from demon-possessed people just by commanding them in the name of Jesus. As much as you give chance to the Holy Spirit to speak (prayer and praise) through you, you will receive that much anointing of God with solid power of the Holy Spirit to glorify the Father and the Son. We need this anointing of the Holy Spirit to bear witness about Jesus too.

Some people thought that tongues of the Spirit are only the gifts of the Holy Spirit. First, tongues of the Spirit are the initial sign of the Holy Spirit. Second, it is the gift of the Holy Spirit that you can receive at the time of your Spirit baptism with other gifts. One can receive more than one gift of the Holy Spirit. If you allow the Holy Spirit to speak through you as I said, you will find out soon that most of the gifts of the Holy Spirit are working through you. I found it in my own life many times. Tongues of the Spirit are the powerful double-edged sword that can cast the demons, heal the sick, break the curses, and bless us abundantly. The princes of the world (demons) cannot understand the tongues of the Holy Spirit, but they can run away because of the power of the tongues of the Spirit.

The tongues of the Spirit perfectly edifies us personally, because He uses the new tongues to empower us. Spiritually we become powerful by giving the Spirit chance to speak through us.

The Holy Spirit is omnipresent, and when we give Him the chance to speak through us He can help others by interceding through our mouths. So the Holy Spirit can intercede through us if we give Him the chance to speak through us. Even prophecies come through the tongues of the Spirit, and the Spirit gives interpretation to others to build His church.

Tongues of the Spirit open the door for us to use the gifts of the Holy Spirit:

> But the manifestation of the Spirit is given to each one for the profit of all: for to one is given the word of wisdom through the Spirit, to another the word of knowledge through the same Spirit, to another faith by the same Spirit, to another gifts of healings by the same Spirit, to another the working of miracles, to another prophecy, to another discerning of spirits, to another different kinds of tongues, to another the interpretation of tongues. But one and the same Spirit works all these things, distributing to each one individually as He wills.
>
> —1 CORINTHIANS 12:7–11

When we are practicing the gifts (power) of the Holy Spirit, we are producing the *fruit of the Holy Spirit*:

> But the fruit of the Spirit is love, joy, peace, longsuffering, kindness, goodness, faithfulness, gentleness, self-control. Against such there is no law.
>
> —GALATIANS 5:22–23

When we are able to practice the gifts and produce the fruit of the Holy Spirit, we become like Jesus. So without the born-again experience through the Water and Spirit baptism with the evidence of tongues it is impossible for any believer to become like Jesus. No one is able to use the gifts of the Holy Spirit to produce the fruit of the Holy Spirit without the born-again experience.

The Holy Spirit told us about His specific attributes in Galatians 5:22–23. Each fruit is equal because all nine are the perfect attributes of the Holy Spirit (God). Therefore we must become fruitful, not practicing just one fruit, but all and equally. The Holy Spirit is the One who leads us to bear these nine attributes of Him; he never gives just one fruit. He teaches us how to love others with patience, kindness, goodness, faithfulness, gentleness, and self-control to be loved by Him with true love and intimacy to be filled with joy of our spiritual life and have real peace. All of the fruit of the Holy Spirit is the result of the fullness of the Holy Spirit to become like Jesus.

Human flesh has a lower level of these nine attributes of God, because God created human beings as His own image by His own breath, but they lost it when they separated from God in the Eden Garden. That lower-level fruit can lead them to receive higher-level fruit by the Holy Spirit in Christ, or it can even lead them to improve it with self-pride without the Holy Spirit. I know some Muslims who have a certain degree of love for others that in general people do not have, though they are seriously lacking of the other fruit of the Spirit, which causes them to live with pain, sorrow, and sickness without any hope and peace. Their love is not even the same love of the Holy Spirit that follows through a Spirit-filled human life.

Paul also told about the love in 1 Corinthians 13. Though the postmodern church read it many times in preaching, teaching, and singing, because of the lack of the fullness of the Holy Spirit they are lacking the fruit of the Holy Spirit. Are they trying to improve themselves without the Holy Spirit? One cannot produce any of this fruit with full measure without the fullness of the Holy Spirit. We Christians must try to be filled with the Holy Spirit to bear His fruit, but must not try to produce this fruit through our own flesh and blood (power) by obeying any law or even making them as law.

The gifts of the Holy Spirit are for the church (born-again Christians) for all generations. Until Jesus comes again to take us into heaven with Him we will always have the gifts of the Holy Spirit with us on earth. When the Holy Spirit lives in us we always have the power of God with all of His spiritual gifts to build His church (John 14:12; Eph. 1:20–23). The Holy Spirit is the power of God the Almighty who lives in us; and the demonstrations of His power are the gifts of the Holy Spirit. If a person really has the indwelling Holy Spirit inside of him, he needs to listen to Him—not only to what makes Him happy, but also to be driven by Him. Some people who don't hear the voice of God always talk against the gifts of the Holy Spirit, because they do not understand that it ultimately leads them against God and His power. Who can stand against God? Only Satan and his followers or the foolish ones go against God and His power.

The gifts of the Holy Spirit show the authority of Jesus against the power of the demons and sickness. The gifts of the Holy Spirit are the love of God in action for the lost and needy ones. There are nine gifts of the Holy Spirit that we find in 1 Corinthians 12:8–10: 1) the gifts of wisdom, 2) the gifts of knowledge, 3) the gifts of mighty faith, 4) the gifts of healing to heal sick people, 5) the gifts of miracles to do miracles, 6) the gifts of prophecy

to give prophecy by the Holy Spirit, 7) the gifts of discernment, 8) the gifts of tongues to speak the languages
of the Holy Spirit, and 9) the gifts of the interpretation of
the tongues of the Holy Spirit.

All of these gifts work by the Holy Spirit. His presence,
His voice, His power, His faith, His wisdom, His knowledge, and His languages are the sources for the working/
serving gifts of the Holy Spirit. The Holy Spirit counsels
us to give us His wisdom for our bright future. He tells
us how to do the job successfully—that is His knowledge.
He empowers us and tells us to do certain things with
boldness—that is the gift of mighty faith. He gives us the
power to heal, and tells us whom are going to heal if we
touch or pray or even ask to God to heal them.

In 1997, I went to a city for a youth revival and healing
meeting. After my preaching the Holy Spirit told me to
tell everyone to remove their powered glasses by faith to
receive healing for their eyes. There were many who used
power glasses to see, but at that very moment when they
removed their glasses by faith by hearing my word that I
heard from the Holy Spirit, all of their eyes were healed.

In 1995, one man came to me who was sick with blood
cancer, and his doctor had given him a date for his death.
When I prayed for him, the Holy Spirit told me He would
heal the man within one month, but he needs to shape
his life and live for Him. He did, and was healed. He is
still living healthy. Last year (2013) he came to meet with
me.

The Holy Spirit told me who is living and leading by
which type of spirits—that is discernment from the Holy
Spirit. One Catholic man was doing healing ministry
with Catholic prayers in his home. The Holy Spirit told
me that he was doing all those healing and sin-telling

things by the jinnes (evil spirits). I casted the jinnes out of him and his ministry stopped as the Holy Spirit told me.

One single mother came to me for a miracle because her son was lost for two weeks. When I prayed with them the Holy Spirit told me that her son would come back within three days. I told her what I heard from the Holy Spirit, and her son really came back on the afternoon of the third day. Her ten-year-old son had been stolen by a group who sell human body parts to the rich people. The day before his surgery an unknown man who fed him helped him to be free. The boy told his mother that this man was an angel.

I have been practicing the gifts of tongues abundantly since I was born again. The first time, I went to a Pentecostal Holiness Church in Fontana, California. After worship, a man of God gave a prophecy with tongues, and the Holy Spirit gave me the interpretation of it in my chest with burning to deliver it. I interpreted the prophecy of tongues. I have been practicing the gifts of the Holy Spirit since 1995. I can tell thousands of stories, one after another, how the Holy Spirit used me to practice the gifts of the Holy Spirit.

Warning: Satan can possess people to use them to manifest their power. Witchcraft and black magic are active on earth through the power of the demons. So be careful! Don't go against the power of the Holy Spirit and His gifts.

Please don't be deceived by any false teaching that cannot give you complete assurance to enter into heaven. If you need help to receive complete assurance to enter into heaven, please contact your pastor or anyone who already knows how to enter into heaven. Or call/e-mail us for an appointment. Our team at Heaven For You, Inc. is available to help you enter into heaven.

This is the complete assurance to enter into heaven to live with God! Enjoy now your new life by living through the Spirit of God.

God bless you with your personal born-again experience, which can lead you to have true peace because you are not going to hell anymore! Now you can listen to the Holy Spirit because He is living in you—that's why you are a born-again Christian. Again, you can listen to His voice because the Holy Spirit is living in you to talk with you. And you can obey His voice because He is the power of God who lives in you to empower you always, forever and ever. In the almighty precious name of Jesus, amen.

In John 14:1–3, Jesus declared:

> "Don't let your hearts be troubled. Trust in God, and trust also in me. There is more than enough room in my Father's home. If this were not so, would I have told you that I am going to prepare a place for you? When everything is ready, I will come and get you, so that you will always be with me where I am."

With Jesus's love and fellowship through His Spirit, the Holy Spirit,

Rev. Isaac William King

President/CEO, Heaven For You, Inc.

Pastor, Living Church of Jesus

E-mail: isaacking100@yahoo.com

http://www.revisaacwilliamking.com

NOTES

3: JESUS IS GOD

1. Millard J. Erickson, *Christian Theology* (Grand Rapids, MI: Baker Academic, 1998), 363.

5: THE LOVE AND GRACE OF GOD ARE ONLY FOUND IN JESUS CHRIST

1. Henry Cloud, *Changes That Heal: How to Understand Your Past to Ensure a Healthier Future* (Grand Rapids, MI: Zondervan,1992), 19.

6: LOVE VS. LAW

1. "Born Again (1979) by Dr. Billy Graham," 2011, video clip, accessed June 5, 2014, YouTube, https://www.youtube.com/watch?feature=player_embedded&v=B9fE5GZvBGk.

12: BE SURE OF YOUR SALVATION

1. Rev. Isaac King, *Complete Assurance to Enter into Heaven* (Denver, CO: Outskirts Press, Inc., 2010), 152–154.

13: EVIDENCES OF BEING BORN AGAIN TO ENTER INTO HEAVEN

1. Howard M. Ervin, *Spirit Baptism: A Biblical Investigation* (Peabody, MA: Hendrickson Publishers, Inc., 1987), 71.
2. Ibid., 76.
3. Ibid., 79.
4. Vinson Synan, *The Holiness-Pentecostal Tradition: Charismatic Movements in the Twentieth Century* (Grand Rapids, MI: William B. Eerdmans Publishing Company, 1997), 92.
5. Ibid., 99–100.
6. Vinson Synan, *The Century of the Holy Spirit: 100 Years of Pentecostal and Charismatic Renewal* (Dallas, TX: Thomas Nelson, 2001), 1.
7. Vinson Synan, *The Holiness-Pentecostal Tradition*, 96.
8. Ibid., 96.
9. Ibid., 145.
10. Ibid., 101.
11. Ibid., 112.
12. Jack Hayford, *Spirit-Filled: The Overflowing Power of the Holy Spirit* (Wheaton, IL: Tyndale House Publishers, Inc., 1987), 84–85.

13.   Veli-Matti Kärkkäinen, *Pneumatology* (Grand Rapids, MI: Baker Academic, 2002), 96.

14.   Ava Stallings, "2 Peter 1:3," (lecture presented in the online class, Pentecostal Charismatic Movement, The King's University, Van Nuys, CA, March 13, 2013), 2.

15.   Charles Caldwell Ryrie, *The Holy Spirit* (Chicago: Moody Press, 1965), 89.

16.   Ava Stallings, "2 Peter 1:3 is the citation of which I have used a portion in this statement," 1.

17.   Paul Yonggi Cho, *The Holy Spirit, My Senior Partner: Understanding the Holy Spirit and His Gifts* (Altamonte Springs, FL: Creation House, 1989), 117.

18.   J. Dwight Pentecost, *The Words and Works of Jesus Christ* (Grand Rapids, MI: Zondervan, 1981), 511.

19.   Howard M. Ervin, *Spirit Baptism*, 101.

BIBLIOGRAPHY

Cho, Paul Yonggi. *The Holy Spirit, My Senior Partner: Understanding the Holy Spirit and His Gifts.* Altamonte Springs, FL: Creation House, 1989.

Cloud, Henry. *Changes That Heal: How to Understand Your Past to Ensure a Healthier Future.* Grand Rapids, MI: Zondervan, 1992.

Erickson, Millard J. *Christian Theology.* Grand Rapids, MI: Baker Academic, 1998.

Ervin, Howard M. *Spirit Baptism: A Biblical Investigation.* Peabody, MA: Hendrickson Publishers, Inc., 1987.

Hayford, Jack. *Spirit-Filled: The Overflowing Power of the Holy Spirit.* Wheaton, IL: Tyndale House Publishers, Inc., 1987.

Kärkkäinen, Veli-Matti. *Pneumatology.* Grand Rapids, MI: Baker Academic, 2002.

King, Rev. Isaac. *Complete Assurance to Enter into Heaven.* Denver, CO: Outskirts Press, Inc., 2010.

Pentecost, J. Dwight. The Words and Works of Jesus Christ. Grand Rapids, MI: Zondervan, 1981.

Ryrie, Charles Caldwell. *The Holy Spirit.* Chicago: Moody Press, 1965.

Stallings, Ava. "2 Peter 1:3." Lecture presented in the online class, Pentecostal Charismatic Movement, The King's University, Van Nuys, CA, March 13, 2013.

Synan, Vinson. *The Holiness-Pentecostal Tradition: Charismatic Movements in the Twentieth Century.* Grand Rapids, MI: William B. Eerdmans Publishing Company, 1971, 1997.

Synan, Vinson. *The Century of the Holy Spirit: 100 Years of Pentecostal and Charismatic Renewal.* Dallas, TX: Thomas Nelson, 2001.

ABOUT THE AUTHOR'S MINISTRY

H EAVEN FOR YOU Ministries has been working among the Muslims in Muslim countries. By God's grace, thousands of Muslims have already come to Jesus through this ministry, and hundreds of new churches have already been planted among them. I request that you prayerfully consider giving a generous donation into this ministry, where your money will be used to save the lost souls, especially among the Muslims. If you have any questions, please feel free to contact us: http://www .revisaacwilliamking.com/heaven-for-you-ministries .html.

God bless you abundantly in Christ. Shalom!

When Jesus is born in us by the Holy Spirit we become born again to live with Him in heaven forever.

Amen.

CONTACT THE AUTHOR

E-mail: isaacking100@yahoo.com

http://www.revisaacwilliamking.com

www.isaacking.us

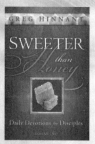